Afield

Afield

FORTY YEARS OF BIRDING THE AMERICAN WEST

Alan Contreras
illustrated by
Ramiel Papish

Oregon State University Press
Corvallis

About the art
Front cover: Varied Thrush painting by Ramiel Papish

The art of Ramiel Papish is available from the artist as originals,
cards, and prints from www.rampapish.com

The paper in this book meets the guidelines for permanence and
durability of the Committee on Production Guidelines for Book
Longevity of the Council on Library Resources and the minimum
requirements of the American National Standard for Permanence of
Paper for Printed Library Materials Z39.48-1984.

Library of Congress Cataloging-in-Publication Data
Contreras, Alan, 1956-
  Afield : forty years of birding the American West / Alan Contreras ;
illustrated by Ramiel Papish.
      p. cm.
  Includes bibliographical references and index.
  ISBN 978-0-87071-420-7 (alk. paper)
  1. Birds--West (U.S.)--Anecdotes. 2. Bird watching--West (U.S.)--
Anecdotes. I. Title.
  QL683.W4C66 2009
  598'.07'23478--dc22

First published in 2009 by Oregon State University Press
Printed in the United States of America

Oregon State University Press
121 The Valley Library
Corvallis OR 97331-4501
541-737-3166 • fax 541-737-3170
http://oregonstate.edu/dept/press

Dedication

For Thelma Greenfield, whose lifelong friendship means so much, and to the memory of Stanley Greenfield, whose thoughtful kindness and good humor is missed.

The Lover of Nature
by Edward A. Preble

To the nature lover the universe constantly pours out its wealth. Daily he gathers the fruits of seed sown in the beginning of the world.

For him no season is dull, for each is successively absorbing: In Spring he is entranced by the awakening of myriad forms of life; Summer reveals the maturity of all creation; Autumn brings the fulfillment of earlier promises; Winter lulls life to sleep, with its assurance of the resurrection.

All weathers are one: The rains of Spring nourish all nature; the heats of Summer mature and ripen its fruits; the frosts of Winter give rest and peace; in all he rejoices.

Each day is good: In the morning life awakens with him; through the noon it works; the peace and quiet of evening shed their benediction upon him.

He knows no dull moments; he seeks not to hurry time. If he be delayed, he may discover something never before seen by man, and his impatience is forgotten.

His youth is filled with the joys of discovery; in middle age the marvels about him hold his interest undimmed; he awaits old age with calmness, for he is one with the universe, and is content.

"The Lover of Nature," early twentieth century by Edward A. Preble, reprinted in *Early Twentieth Century Ornithology in Malheur County, Oregon*, Noah Strycker, ed., 2003, p. 155.

Contents

Preface 10

Prologue 11

1960: The Green Coast 12

1967: "Would you like to go look at birds?" 14

1969: Far Eastern Oregon 22

1970: The Great Pilgrimage 31

1975: Childhood's End 44

1976: The First Big Day 52

1985: Steens Mountain 54

1986–1991: The Mountains of Home 59

1993: The Music of the Stars 69

1994: A Missourian Visits the West 74

1995: Valleys in the Sun 82

1999: Listing for a Purpose 90

1999: California Gulch 100

2000: Everything's Big in Texas 103

2000: The Importance of "Yet" 109

2003: Just a Long Weekend 114

2003: Everything Flies in Alaska 119

The Next Bird 129

Epilogue: Germany, 1944/Oregon 2002: *Tod und Verklärung* 134

Acknowledgements and Derivations 135

Recommended Reading 137

Principal Locations Mentioned in the Text 137

Index 139

Preface

This collection is intended to bring to its readers a sense of how I have enjoyed the natural world of Oregon and the West, in which I have spent so many rewarding hours for the past forty years. I write largely from the perspective of a birder, but this collection is also about people and how they perceive nature. Most of the essays were written specifically for this book, but a few were revised from other essays, articles and poems that I have published in *Oregon Birds, Fieldwork* and other venues.

I am a writer who enjoys birds and the natural world, not a biologist who writes. For this reason, you will find more of wonder than of science in this book, though I have made every effort to provide an accurate depiction of the places and wildlife that I have observed.

This is not exactly a history, a personal memoir, or a birding adventure book, though it offers elements of all three. It is only in part a natural history in the usual sense of the term. It is a record of my beginnings and growth as an observer of the natural world and of the people who have shared my interest.

In order to provide some context to the story, I have occasionally used the comments of ornithologists and other early explorers in the region as a way of establishing both a natural and a literary baseline for the region and its natural wonders.

Finally, it is in the largest sense a love story, a story of joy and of loss, and, I hope, a reaffirmation of the value of individual, unhurried observation of the world around us.

Alan Contreras
Eugene, Oregon, August, 2008

Prologue

For thirty-four years I had waited for the day and now, on my home stretch of the Oregon coast, it was at hand. For a birder who keeps lists, one of the ultimate pleasures is to find a first state record, such as the Falcated Duck that appeared with an escort of twelve Eurasian Wigeon at Fern Ridge Dam in western Oregon in January 2004. I wish I had found it. To be sure, there are other kinds of records to be had, since birders dream up potential lists with great creativity: year lists, location lists, county lists, and so on. But to be the first person to record the sighting of a species in the state is the gold standard.

From the time I started birding in 1967 through late 2000—almost thirty-four years—I had never found a first state record. I had certainly *seen* some found by others, a joy not to be despised, but had never found any myself. I had managed to find some *second* state records, some of which were spectacular in their own way, such as the Rusty Blackbird at Baskett Slough National Wildlife Refuge in November 1977, which was first spotted by Kathy Finnell, but which I was among the first to identify as it poked around in a muddy field with other blackbirds. It had been eighteen years since the first record of Rusty Blackbird, so that felt pretty good at the time. The Bell's Vireo at Fields Oasis in the Alvord Desert was another excellent second record, as was the Worm-eating Warbler at Malheur headquarters in June 2001.

But before we find our first state record together, why was I even out there? Why did I want to see these birds at all? The transition from a child vaguely interested in the natural world to one pursuing unusual birds had many phases. That is what this book is about, in part. But first, forty years before that glorious day back at the coast, a small boy slid down the sand dunes of Oregon.

1960: The Green Coast

For beauty of background and for a wide sandy stretch of matchless beach there is no place on the whole Pacific Coast can equal the ocean front of Nehalem. The mountain, rising in easy terraces from the water's edge, forms a background that rivals any on earth. Somehow or other, nature carpeted this slope with eternal green, and the alluvial deposits from the centuries of transformation of the mountain side has built a soil that can be equalled (sic) nowhere else along the ocean.

Gradually decreasing in its ability to sustain life, it finally ends in pure sand far down the coast line in Nehalem Spit, a point of land forming a barrier between the ocean and Nehalem Bay. From Neahkahnie to the mouth of the river is five miles of broad beach. Differing from that of other sections along the coast, the slope of the beach is gradual, and at low tide several hundred feet in width. The surf along this beach is just the right strength for bathing, and hundreds of people delight in a cool dip during the continual pleasant weather of summer.

Stories of Nehalem, Sam J. Cotton, 1915, p. 139-40

Eternal green. That is as good a memory as any, given that our yard was walled in by a stand of Douglas-fir and a huckleberry hedge, perhaps two miles from the lower slopes of Neahkahnie Mountain. I suppose it was 1960 when I first made a meaningful excursion outside the yard in Manzanita. It was a long while ago and I do not know how old I was when I became truly mobile. There is no one to ask.

The yard itself held some limited flora and fauna, to be sure. In the category of flora, I remember only the huckleberry hedge down which a willing picker, even four years old, could profitably wander, absorbing sweet berries all the way. The deep green leaves glistened with a solid, practical sheen. No flashy overdone colors or attitudes here—these were huckleberries, the solid citizens of Oregon coastal shrubbery, not picky, flash-in-the-pan blueberries eager to show off their carmine finery in October, or even worse, cranberries imprisoned in their sterile waffles of bare dirt.

The principal hazard to a four-year-old picker of huckleberries on Third Street was an apparition known as Jiggs, though why it held that odd name I never knew. Jiggs was a boxer, the canine kind, an immense loping tan hound that moved with disturbing silence from the neighbor's house to our lawn, appearing to my eyes the size of a middle-sized moose, but with sharper teeth. I did not see a real moose for another forty years, but in 1960, Jiggs sufficed.

For defense against the always-imminent horror of Jiggs our family had a shaggy black spaniel with the equally improbable name of Sprouts and a marmot-like gait. To this day I can't remember a single interaction between them, the sole examples of memorable non-human fauna present in the yard. I suspect that Sprouts always chose discretion and did not notice when Jiggs made one of his frequent *in terrorem* passages through the yard.

When I was about four I left the yard behind and went to the ocean, a salmon-like migration that I have repeated all of my life. Granted, from Third Street in Manzanita to the ocean is only about half a mile, and I had probably been taken there before, but it is from age four through age six that the experience has remained in my memory. That is because it was during these years that I experienced the dunes.

I visited a section of dunes near Manzanita again in May 2007, and the immense mountains of sand I remember were in roughly the same proportion to their actual size as was Jiggs to a moose, yet my memories are of sitting far, far above my parents on a loose shifting shelf of sand, feeling the smoothness of the granular flow over my hands and feet and noticing how a pattern of grains clung to my legs, a different pattern if I were dry or had been to the water's edge. Then the long slide down the dune face, never quite steep enough yet capable of engendering wild careening.

These dunes were not far from Neahkahnie Mountain, which loomed over the town, our misty Gibraltar, rumored site of lost treasure. On its southern slope highway 101 labored upward so steeply that my most memorable faunistic experience occurred not at home or on the dunes, but standing by the highway with half the town watching a traveling circus go up the hill.

This circus traveled in trucks, but no one had told the manager (what does one call the head of a circus? Ringmaster conjures up images of Frodo and Gandalf) that 101 was not designed with such trucks in mind. In fact, the elephant trucks were far too heavy, so the town of Manzanita was witness to the neo-Jurassic sight of elephants unloaded and employed in the curiously Himalayan exercise of pushing the trucks uphill over Neahkahnie Mountain. Today I imagine the ghost of Hannibal nodding with approval from atop some rocky spur.

1967: "Would you like to go look at birds?"

We moved from the coast to Dallas, Oregon, when I was six years old. Dallas was very close to where my mother grew up and in our trips back and forth to her parents' place south of Salem I first became conscious of wildlife slightly more native than elephants: Ring-necked Pheasants and Northern Bobwhite. At least they had been here longer and were breeding in the wild. The pheasants would have felt more at home with the elephants than dodging cows in the Willamette Valley, since they are native to Asia. The Bobwhite were at least native to North America, and in those years we saw them fairly often in the fields and hedgerows east of Dallas, where introduced populations were doing reasonably well. Today they no longer occur in Oregon except as escapes or releases from hunt clubs.

These years, the early 1960s, were the last years that original populations of Sharp-tailed Grouse were found in the wild in Oregon. As I was learning the difference between Bobwhite (brown with vestigial crest) and California Quail (absurd waving question mark on its head) in the north valley, the last Sharp-tails were fading into Lookout Mountain, three hundred miles to the east in Baker County. I did not know there was such a thing as a grouse, for I was not really a birder then, just someone whose mother knew the local fowl from her years growing up on farms.

In Dallas I saw birds and occasionally other wildlife along Rickreall Creek, at the edge of the schoolyard at Lyle school, and in the small park near our house. My most vivid memory from Dallas may be the week that I managed to lose two kites the same way in the same place. I had never had a kite before and now I had none, twice over. I cried and thought I was destined for endless sorrow. Is there any pain equal to that of a child?

The friends I made there, Becky Sapp, Jack Scott, Lynn Courtney, and others have names that have passed into the mist, for it was not easy for ten-year-olds to stay in touch in 1966, and is only slightly easier today. I saw Jack when we were in our late twenties and he was

The author at about age 11, binoculars not visible

doing fine. I saw Lynn's photo once when he, then a police officer, was involved in smiting the wicked.Somehow the intense desire to be friends forever comes with the teenage years, not the single digits; those we know in childhood remain part of a distant, unreachable summer, for it is always summer in my memories of that childhood.

When we moved from Dallas to Eugene in late 1966 I did not know that I was about to fall into the spell of watching birds, let alone that there was such a thing as a dotterel. I say "into" rather than "under" because to this day I have a sensation of being caught up in a fantasia of wildness that continues to swirl, reconceiving my life's boundaries each day.

Sayre Greenfield, whom I met in Gale Taylor's fifth grade class, would be a lifelong friend and co-conspirator, but at age eleven I did not know this. We did not, right away, know that we were born the very same day on opposite sides of the continent. In fact we knew each other for nearly a year before that fact came up.

The years of high adventure within a few miles of our homes, the play-reading parties, the surrogate role his parents Stanley and Thelma would play in my life as more than honorary aunt and uncle, all of these things were not in our minds at all when we were just eleven. That he, with an early affinity for mathematics, would marry Linda Troost, an elegant beauty of Estonian ancestry, and become an English professor in Pennsylvania, where I could see him but rarely, we did not know. That I would become psychologically rooted in Oregon, a mediocre law student and successful bureaucrat, of this we had no idea.

Most of all, could we have imagined then that thirty-six years later I would co-edit the definitive update of *Birds of Oregon* and dedicate my work to him? All we knew in that child's spring of 1967 is that I was in a new town, a new school where the kids already knew each other, and that there was nothing in particular for eleven-year-olds to do. Out we went and to our amazement there were *all sorts of birds* right in our neighborhoods.

We lived about five blocks from each other in a very woodsy part of Eugene, each of us adjacent to a city park. In Washburn Park, where I first looked for birds on my own, I saw a Red-breasted Sapsucker and a Red-shafted Flicker, found a White-breasted Nuthatch nest (in a part of town where they rarely occurred then or now), and carefully identified a flock of Cedar Waxwings as titmice (I cannot abide the technically correct Titmouses), using the Peterson western guide, which hid the subtle

Sayre Greenfield at eighteen

glory of waxwings in line art off the main plates. I still have that book today, the only bird book not stolen in 1970 as we prepared to move back to the valley from Nyssa. It was in my bedroom until the last minute, while the two full boxes of bird books were in the garage overnight—a night that lasted forever, as it turned out.

Those early years in Eugene were full of surprises. One day I saw an adult Bald Eagle flying directly toward the playground at Condon School (now Agate Hall, part of the University of Oregon, where Vaux's Swifts gather in migration). As it neared, it shrank a bit, becoming a crow with some kind of white paper cup in its beak. There were better surprises: the day we saw a Western Bluebird in Hendricks Park near Sayre's house, and the days we had our first good looks at Bewick's Wren and "Audubon's" Yellow-rumped Warbler. We met the warbler and birder Margaret Markley at about the same time, as she discovered us peering into her back yard with binoculars. In the winter of 1968-69, Bohemian Waxwings invaded western Oregon in numbers not seen since and I was able to photograph some at point-blank range with my little Kodak Instamatic while walking to Sayre's house.

Most of all, our rickety back porch in 1967 offered a view of the corner of the eaves where the overhang had broken enough to allow a pair of Violet-green Swallows to nest below the gutter. With my

A Note from Sayre

I had, in the most minor way, begun birdwatching (no one "birded" then!) in 1965, though I may have gotten the Peterson western field guide as a present as early as 1964. But I didn't keep records or actually "go" birdwatching. I remember, however, when my family was heading for that first year in England in August of 1965, and we drove up to Vancouver BC and took the train across Canada, seeing Common Loons on the lakes from the train. Then from Montreal we drove south through Vermont, stopping at the village (Wheelock) where my parents had owned a small summer house when we lived in New York City. Here I saw a Great Blue Heron and Cedar Waxwings.

These are about the first specific birds I remember, outside of a Blue Jay on a visit back to my grandparents in 1962. I was sitting in my grandfather's lap as he was driving the car, and he "let" six-year old me "drive" the car for a minute, except this jay flew across the highway, and I wanted to look at that, not the road. Also, somewhere in the 1962-64 range, I saw a Steller's Jay at a lunch table on the southern Oregon coast.

The real moment of birding for me came in April 1966. When we had arrived in England the previous autumn, I quickly had my parents buy me a bird book, and I was aware of Blue Tits and Great Tits and House Sparrows and this huge green and purple bird that I finally identified as a Starling (when you're young, gloss counts!). But in April my parents had dumped us in a boarding house while they went off to Paris for a week. Out in the back yard, I saw a pair of Bullfinches and said to myself, "These are so great, I must write this down." And then I started trying to write a list of all the birds I could think of that I had seen in England.

Strangely enough, when I got back to the U.S., I didn't continue listing until we saw the fateful White-breasted Nuthatch with its nest in that weeping willow in Washburn Park. Only then, reinforced by the Western Bluebird in Hendricks Park, did the real fanaticism and proper listing (or at least the days on which I first saw a bird) begin. Interestingly, I have a precise date for the bluebird, not the nuthatch. So that's how I got started a-birding.— Sayre Greenfield glorious Tasco 6x30 binoculars (not bad in 1968, though I don't know how my mother afforded them) I was able to see every feather on them as they came and went, showing their unlikely colors to full advantage. Today I live less than a mile from that house, and each year a pair of Violet-greens nests in a box above my driveway. I like to think that there is some linear connection, some slender twist of DNA, running through time and these swallows.

During these years we discovered the pleasures of Fern Ridge Reservoir, where we saw Oregon's second White-tailed Kite, an unbearably exotic ghost image hovering at the very edge of our optical capacity. There was also a Swamp Sparrow one winter—considered very rare then, but like the kite, regular in western Oregon now. In December of 1968, right before an unprecedented three feet of snow collapsed the city, an immature Swainson's Hawk was enjoyed by many of us as it looked down from its perch by the reservoir—none was to appear again near Eugene in winter until 2005.

Birding was done mainly around town, but that was pretty exciting for a child to whom *most* birds offered new experiences. Almost anything could be in local parks, and when I started going to seventh

Sayre Greenfield (left) and the author, June 2006
(Photo by Tamma Greenfield)

grade at Roosevelt Junior High, opportunity was right there in the form of a narrow ditch that drained into Amazon Creek. This ditch is now covered by playing fields, but in spring 1969 it contained something very exciting, then called a Long-billed Marsh Wren, now reduced in glory to mere Marsh Wren, though its bill is as long as ever.

From spring 1968 through June 1969, Sayre and I produced a mimeographed bird newsletter called *The Meadowlark*. Somehow we managed to find something to write about every two weeks, give or take. We produced thirty-four issues in a little over a year. At this time there was no Audubon Society in the Eugene area, though the Eugene Natural History Society had been operating since 1941. *The Meadowlark* was a bird newsletter that chronicled our own sightings and travels, with a few other items.

When we were in the seventh grade at Roosevelt, teachers and even vice-principal Don Jackson (later to be a well-known high school principal in the area) were known to blanch in realization—too late—when they saw us coming with a few copies of *The Meadowlark*, because we *charged* for it, three cents. They could hardly refuse us and discourage our writing experience, so they paid and paid and paid. If any of them read this, I hope they will consider it an improvement.

Note to rare-book collectors: one of the thirty-four issues spelled the name "Meadolark" without a "w" on the hand-lettered masthead. I'm sure it is worth double the original face value today.

These years also took me farther afield: watching California Towhees and Anna's Hummingbirds at my uncle Gary Barker's house in Alameda, California, flushing a Common Poorwill while fishing at Haystack Reservoir in eastern Oregon with my aunt Jeannette. This was the all-too-memorable summer of 1968, when at age twelve I was aware of the horrors going on in Vietnam and Hungary, to say nothing of the United States, but was not yet sufficiently connected with the world of people to think much about them. I was thinking about birds.

The poet James Merrill, a favorite of mine, is said never to have read a newspaper or voted, being devoted to poetry and the opera. That is how I was in those formative years of my devotion to birding. In the summer of 1968 I was starting to realize just how much there was to the world of birds, and no images of tanks or tear gas distracted me for long. As far as I knew, Alexander Dubcek, alive, dead, or in prison could not tell me anything about Lincoln's Sparrow, nor could Richard Nixon: I was focused.

Three Arch Rocks

Three Arch Rocks was among the first "exotic" locales I visited as a pre-teen birdwatcher. My great-uncle Lyle Kirk owned Kirk's Oceanside Cottages in the town of Oceanside just south of Cape Meares, and from the town and the adjacent beach, the rocks commanded the western horizon. The fecundity of the rocks in summer are described no better than this:

These were Isles of Life. Here, in the rocky caverns, was conceived and brought forth a life as crude and raw and elemental as the rock itself. It covered every crag. I clutched it in my hands; I crushed it under my feet; it was thick in the air about me. My narrow path up the face of the rock was a succession of sea-bird rookeries, of crowded eggs, and huddled young, hairy or naked or wet from the shell.

Every time my fingers felt for a crack overhead, they touched something warm that rolled or squirmed; every time my feet moved under me for a hold, they pushed in among top-shaped eggs that turned on the shelf or went over far below; and whenever I hugged the pushing wall I must bear off from a mass of squealing, struggling, shapeless things, just hatched.

And down upon me, as rookery after rookery of old birds whirred in fright from their ledges, fell crashing eggs and unfledged young, that the greedy gulls devoured ere they touched the sea.

Where Rolls the Oregon, Dallas Lore Sharp, 1914, p. 18-19.

During our summer visits after moving to Dallas in 1962 and Eugene in 1966, I used my very basic binoculars (Tasco 6x30s, unearthed to my astonishment in 2004 from my brother's closet) to watch the distant murres swarming about their colony. Puffins were hard to spot unless I used the monster telescope built onto a nearby deck.

The north coast of Oregon in late summer is both a huge tourist attraction and one of the great beautiful places of the nation. The crucial Oregon law declaring the beaches to be public land accessible to all (through the simple action of declaring the beach a public highway) has prevented the development of private walled enclaves as occurs in California and elsewhere.For this reason, tourists of all kinds simply mingle in a great spray of public parks and campgrounds all along the coast, walking the beaches in the misty dawn, building sand

Tufted Puffins, Brandt's and Pelagic Cormorants and Common Murres at a coastal colony. Ramiel Papish

castles, and watching the sun pass beyond Three Arch Rocks, beyond Haystack Rock, beyond the swarming gulls, finally beyond the day itself, rising in Japan seven thousand miles away while a thousand campfires commemorate its passing.

It is the narrow bar of more-or-less impassable ocean that allows the huge seabird colonies to survive and, in some years, flourish, right next to the tourist towns, so that teenagers can still gaze spellbound at the murre colonies, the extraordinary tuft-graced faces of the puffins, the unlikely love of a mother cormorant for its reptilian young and the glaring red lining of a guillemot's mouth.

In recent years, the expansion of Bald Eagle as a breeder along the Oregon coast has caused many nesting failures at murre colonies. Even when the eagles are unsuccessful in hunting, the massive disruption caused by thousands of seabirds erupting away from the rocks on a regular basis effectively precludes successful breeding by the seabirds, especially murres. The eventual outcome of this perfectly natural change in avifaunal habits is not yet known; surely it is an unlikely picture to imagine wildlife managers chasing off Bald Eagles that they once tried to attract, yet we have seen stranger happenings. Today we read of plans to systematically kill Barred Owls in a probably hopeless attempt to permanently preserve the northern subspecies of the Spotted Owl.

1969: Far Eastern Oregon

In the summer of 1969 I was thirteen years old and had been birding for two years. We moved to Nyssa, Oregon, for a year, far from my birding friends, and to indulge my mother I reluctantly joined the eighth-grade basketball team. The coach accepted me as a sort of mascot, since I was unsuited by physiognomy, attitude, altitude, and skill for basketball. I recall scoring a free throw that year after someone ran into me during one of my brief stretches of playing time. On the other hand, that could just be a persistent dream.

That year in Nyssa allowed me to see Bobwhite, which was introduced in the area, though it is essentially absent today, as well as Chukars, Gray Partridge, and a plethora of pheasants. We lived in the country for a few months in a house rented from the Esplin family, where our elderly yet fecund cat Chalcedony finally met her match when she assaulted a cock Ring-necked Pheasant. This was a bird far above her station as a modest house cat. She captured a few gorgeous feathers and returned the worse for wear to die a couple of days later, perhaps from embarrassment. My best bird memory of that time, however, is the perfect feather-print left by a Barn Owl that had whumped into the front window at low speed with wings outspread, leaving a ghost image of itself behind as it flew off.

That year in Nyssa is itself a kind of ghost image now, thirty-eight years later, with visions of overheated youth mixed with memories of things that may or may not have happened. Manuel Perez, elected class president in that faraway world, definitely existed; I met him during college and he is now a lawyer in Ontario. When Nyssa reached the state basketball championships in 1974, I was able to say hello again to star player Philip Klinkenberg after the game at the University of Oregon's McArthur Court, near where I lived. His memory of me was much like mine of Nyssa: vaguely pleasant but not requiring a lot of attention. Where today are friendly Mike Stringer, warm Cor Hopman, quietly welcoming Scott Blaylock? Lives move in one direction, memories remain as they were.

After we moved into the town of Nyssa, birding was more limited, but as an antidote to boredom and the strange chemical urges of age thirteen, I discovered and often embarked on what I came to call the river walk, even though it was mostly walk and little river. We lived perhaps half a mile from the Snake River, on First Street next to Frank and Lupe Grimaldo's family, wonderful people with whom I was to spend the summer of 1970 hoeing in the beet and potato fields, earning money for my first camera. That camera, to which I optimistically affixed a label saying "The Confirmer," confirmed only one unusual bird in its long life, a Sage Thrasher that Clare Watson found in the University of Oregon cemetery.

A couple of blocks to the south of our home there was a street that ran quickly out of town to the east, becoming a gravel road that led through agricultural land. These fields were where I first discovered the peculiar pleasures of watching pipits.

The American Pipit is a small, rather plain-looking bird that walks about on bare ground or in open grassy areas, bobbing its tail up and down while exuding an air of purposeful searching. The thousands I have seen never seem to actually find what they are looking for.

Barn Owls. Ramiel Papish

For purposeful searching, though, they are without peer in the avian world.

On my river walk behind Nyssa at age thirteen I watched a lot of pipits while becoming accustomed to the too-rich smells coming from the sugar beet plant and the nearby farms. These pipits generally came in flocks of twenty to forty birds, and as the river mist rose they would suddenly be there, as though they had come up from the earth rather than down from the sky. As I watched there would be a sudden sense that the furrows were infested with some kind of Nessie-like serpent whose loose coils were mostly subsurface but which made occasional appearances. As the pipits came closer they could be seen as birds, working along the low ridges and valleys of the freshest turned earth, looking for insects.

From time to time they would fly up and circle about, though they tended to fly off before landing, unlike longspurs that often go around and around in circles before returning to the same place they started out. Even on cold days when not much could be found, I often heard the pipit flocks as they crossed overhead making their "teep! ... tippit!" calls.

These fields did not harbor much else, though from time to time an American Tree Sparrow would creep out from the shelter of the small willows that sprouted here and there. The main purpose of the river walk was, of course, to get to the river, where Anything might occur. In fact, the species variety on the river was not that spectacular, though small numbers of Canada Geese, Mallards, Green-winged Teal, and other waterfowl were usually present.

The prize of these days of escape was always the goldeneyes. Both species winter on the Snake River at Nyssa, but it was a good day when I could find both after reaching the hummocky bluff along the river. More often there would be a few Commons way over on the Idaho side, or a Barrow's flying by too fast for a good look. On the good days, however, my patient poking along the riverbank produced stunning views of these black-and-white marvels up close.

The swifts of Succor Creek

One of the most memorable outdoor experiences during that year in Nyssa was a family trip with our friends the Linegar family (Leslie now teaches at Ontario High School) down Succor Creek as far as

Leslie Gulch. Succor Creek runs north between the Owyhee canyon and the Idaho border. As we bounced down the rutted gravel road that leads into the canyon I saw my first Common Merganser, which I had somehow not seen around Eugene.

At the time I thought it was very strange that this large, indeed massive, duck was flying along over what appeared to be desert scrub. The creek was barely wide enough for a merganser to turn around in, but as I discovered in subsequent years, these big ducks can live and breed along very small streams. This particular merganser kept right on going down the canyon.

That day I also saw the rock specialists: Rock Wrens and Canyon Wrens abound in the canyon's cornices and crevices. In future years I returned to the canyon several times, though it is nine hours from where I live. In fact, it takes longer to get there from Eugene than it takes to get almost anywhere else in the state, because there is no freeway at all between me and Succor Creek, just close to five hundred miles of plain old highway, some of it mighty twisty.

The canyon lies at about three thousand feet in the Owyhee uplands of far southeastern Oregon. It is about fifteen miles long and at most about one to two hundred yards wide, sometimes much narrower, with high cliffs on both sides for part of its length. These cliffs are escorted by turrets, griffins, and gargoyles of orange, yellow, and reddish rock, home to the aforementioned wrens and to White-throated Swifts, a few Golden Eagles, and the occasional Prairie Falcon.

Although there is much pleasure to be had in watching any of these, it is the swifts that attract most observers. Their speed is astounding as they dash along the cliff face, accelerating without seeming to move their wings any differently than when they were just flickering along. When a bird such as a Merlin accelerates, the motion is accompanied by an extraordinary, highly visible piston-driven wing movement. White-throated Swifts just suddenly go faster as though through simple force of will. Their wings are already almost a blur in basic flight; there must be second- and third-gear blurs, and a pursued-by-falcon overdrive blur, but these distinctions are beyond human ken.

Both at Succor Creek and at Fort Rock in Lake County, Oregon, I have been fortunate to see the startling mating flights of these birds. It typically involves more than two birds, often three, in a combined mating and competitive tumble that resembles nothing so much as a cluster of quivering little black-and-white boomerangs thrown from the top of a cliff, falling straight down from the sky in loose linkage, turning over and over while emitting a curious high-pitched chirping trill. The acrobats sometimes don't break loose from each other until less than ten feet from the ground, at which point they sometimes dash right past startled human observers while climbing back up above the clifftops to make another tumble.

In the late 1990s I had occasion to be at Fort Rock during one of these swift displays. Parked near me was renowned naturalist Jim Anderson, who was among the first to find these big swifts in central Oregon in the 1960s. At one point a mating trio fell to within ten feet of us and the birds dashed between our cars with astonishing agility.

How do we humans appear to these swifts? Is there some kind of low-grade spectral shift or bent parallax when a small bird hurtles past a person at a speed well in excess of one hundred miles per hour? Are we essentially the same as trees or stone pillars at that speed, simply a Type A Obstacle to be avoided? From the point of view of a cliff-nesting swift, is there any meaningful, useful difference between an aspen, a person, and a small stone obelisk, assuming that the latter has no useful nesting cracks? I suspect not. We can hardly be perceived as a predator. My friend Rich Hoyer once had a Magnificent Hummingbird try to feed at his mouth high on an Arizona hillside, but I have not known a swift to attempt to roost in a human pocket. Yet.

Leslie Gulch is a spur off the Succor Creek canyon that drops down to the west and eventually reaches the edge of Owyhee Reservoir. What makes it interesting from an ornithological standpoint is that it lies just below the northern flank of Mahogany Mountain and its western end passes through some loose stands of juniper and mountain mahogany. These stands are the northernmost breeding grounds in southeastern Oregon for Black-throated Gray Warblers.

These warblers are not uncommon in the forests of most of western and south-central Oregon, but it always seems strange to find them blithely going about their business in juniper stands on the edge of the sage desert. Some species of birds use different vegetative types that have a similar physical structure. Good examples include Dusky Flycatcher (drier open forests and shrublands of several types), Brewer's Sparrow (tall sagebrush and dwarf conifers), Marsh Wren (sedges, cattails, beach grass). But the Black-throated Grays of western Oregon are mainly a forest bird. Granted, they use edges

White-throated Swifts. Ramiel Papish

rather than the middle of stands, but usually occur in relatively dense, fairly sizable trees.

In Leslie Gulch (and at Page Springs at the south end of Malheur National Wildlife Refuge) they use rather small junipers set in semi-open xeric parkland, a very different kind of space. These "forest warblers" also use this kind of juniper habitat elsewhere in the southern half of eastern Oregon. Is this separation over time what eventually makes a subspecies from a population, a species from a subspecies? I will not be around long enough to find out, but it seems likely.

There are Western Screech-Owls in these juniper stands as well. I saw one during one of my occasional return trips to the area in 1998; Rich Hoyer called it out in the daytime when he was guiding a tour group on a side trail. Well, perhaps "out" is an overstatement, since the bird remained in the dimness of a juniper most of the time.

At least six species of mice, grasshopper mice, pocket mice, and jumping-mice inhabit these canyons, not to mention a couple of voles and wood-rats, though the landscape seems rather forbidding. Kangaroo rats are here, too. There are even two species of shrew in these desert canyons, though we tend to associate shrews with water and moister habitats. There is definitely enough of a prey base to allow a few screech-owls to make a living.

The Succor Creek road eventually emerges onto the main highway just north of Jordan Valley, though after thunderstorms there are portions of the road that are under water, a reminder that nature does not make adjustments for us, we must do so for her.

From the other side of time

I had not seen the name Frank Grimaldo for twenty-three years until I sat in the bleachers overlooking the graduating Treasure Valley Community College class of 1993. The name, as though written in sunlight in the program, welcomed me back to Malheur County. Frank Grimaldo was one of seventy-two students receiving an Associate of Arts degree that June 11. I had scheduled my birding vacation to allow me to attend the graduation, since I was working for the Oregon Community College Association at the time and wanted to show the flag. As I watched my former neighbor's grandson walk across the stage and receive his degree, I thought of the family.

Summer 1970 was a fourteen-year-old's memory of heat and dust. I had picked beans and berries for many years in the Willamette Valley, but hoeing weeds out of the sugar beet fields of the Snake River valley was hard work, and I was not very good at it. The last time I had seen the elder Frank was when we got paid for our summer's work at a home where everyone but me (despite my surname) spoke Spanish. More than once Frank had gone back over my work and found it not up to the standards expected of the weeding crew. He never complained to me, though his son Jaime, who is my age, tried to show me how to do a better job. I would like to think that I improved by the end of the summer. I doubt it.

It was a summer of distractions in the fields. Horned Larks, pheasants, the occasional Gray Partridge or Bobwhite enlivened the days of weeding. One day as I was waddling down the rows hacking ineffectually at weeds, I hit a long-lost spray canister of some kind that was buried by the dirt. For once my aim, though unintended, was perfect. The canister was punctured just enough and at just the right angle: it took off like a miniature rocket, looped up and then sideways—directly for Jaime's head. The hissing sound warned him and he ducked as it went over him, turned straight up for a moment, then wavered and fell.

As I watched Jaime's nephew get his degree (he would go on to Oregon State University), I hoped that my intervening years as a lobbyist for community colleges and financial aid had somehow helped return a favor to the good family I knew in the long hot summer of 1970. My poem "Fieldwork" ends with a recollection of this time:

One summer, one friend, one year from my life
in the gold valley fields on the Snake River plain,
yet I come back again, for I left something there,
some link, some root, some small private thing

Lost in those fields in the summer of dust and
found nowhere else, so I come, look and hope.

1970: The Great Pilgrimage

There is no place like it. The ultimate pilgrimage for Oregon birders and one that is immensely satisfying for anyone interested in the natural world, Malheur National Wildlife Refuge lies at four thousand feet in the high desert at the northern end of the Great Basin. It is shaped like a giant "T," the Donner und Blitzen River (usually just called the Blitzen) flowing north through the column of the T to join Malheur Lake at the headquarters near the junction. Harney Lake comprises the bulk of the left arm of the T while Malheur Lake forms the right arm.

The Great Basin is sometimes thought of as an empty place, even a sterile place. The desert is neither empty nor sterile, indeed it is full of life adapted to its requirements. A place like Malheur, though, provides that crucial factor, that astonishing change agent, *water*. In some years there isn't much, in other years there is too much. Sir Stephen Spender described his life in the early twentieth century in an autobiography entitled *World Within World*. That title could as well describe the consequence of water in the desert.

I first saw Malheur in the late summer of 1970. Having survived the experience of working as a field hand around Nyssa, I had used my entire earnings, some three hundred dollars, to buy a camera. A real camera, that is, a Hanimex Praktica, a kind of poor-boys' Pentax that would take telephoto lenses if I could afford any. I could not, though a 2x doubler gave me some nominal telephotic capacity. Nonetheless, it was a huge step up from my Kodak Instamatic and I wanted to take bird pictures with it.

There was just one problem: the birds around Nyssa in August are not easy to find or photograph if you are fourteen and have a 100-mm lens. My teacher Irl Nolen had taken me to see stilts and avocets at Fort Boise in southwestern Idaho, but those birds were a bit skittish and I really did want to see Malheur. I needed to find some big obvious birds that would hold still. Malheur has lots of small birds that are hard to see, but it also has some big obvious birds that are, if not quite fixed in place, at least reasonably languid and willing to remain close enough to the car to allow themselves to be photographed. Thus we went off with the Linegar family to visit fabled Malheur.

Fabled Malheur in August of 1970 was characterized mainly by tall grass behind which even large languid birds could hide, and a disheartening number of mosquitoes, all of which behaved as though they had not eaten for weeks. Nonetheless we visited the northern part of the refuge and such delights as American Avocets, Black-necked Stilts, and Sandhill Cranes were photographed after a fashion, as were Black Terns and Willets standing on posts.

In that innocent time, birders (the term was then fairly new) had not yet begun systematically milking the groves of trees at the refuge for eastern vagrants. This tactic became standard procedure by the late 1970s and today it seems that each tree and shrub in the Sacred Grove at headquarters has its own reputation as ancient as Middle Earth, and an accompanying proper name, e.g. The Morning Trees, The Spruce, The Hedge.

After we moved back to the Willamette Valley late in August 1970 and settled in Cottage Grove for two years, I began going to Malheur on a regular basis. These early trips were memorable less for rafts of rarities than for the companionship of other teenagers who were to become lifelong friends. These were mostly friends from school who more or less became birders over the years.

Sayre Greenfield became an English professor but remains a birder, Mike Patterson became a biology teacher and as of this writing is regional editor for Christmas Bird Counts for the Northwest, Mark Williams is a lawyer who does not bird anymore but delights (preens would not be an overstatement) in surprising co-workers with the occasional flyby identification, Carol Cunningham got her PhD in American history and works as a computer system manager. Dinah Ward has her own design firm. Diane Morey is raising a family in Arizona. These, along with my brother John, were the core group of those trips in the early 1970s. That I am still regularly in touch with Sayre, Mike, Mark, and Carol suggests how some of these shared experiences served to link us in a positive way.

A typical trip involved my mother Lona arranging to take off a day or two from her teaching job so that she could stuff a bunch of us into the station wagon and zoom over to the refuge. She earned a couple of nicknames during these years. One was "Wol" after the larger owl in Farley Mowat's book "Owls in the Family," which most of us had read. During those years she wore large round glasses that imparted a certain strigid look, though she could spell better than the most famous Wol, from A.A. Milne's stories. Her other name was "Mario" after race driver Mario Andretti, since she loved to drive fast, which came in handy on the long run across the desert to Malheur.

Since most of us sang in school choirs during those years, we often sang songs during the boring stretches of highway, one of which was the infinitely extendable "Funeral Train." My mother no doubt wondered why we on a couple of occasions intentionally stretched the prolonged sad notes into a sound that resembled nothing so much as a cow giving vent to her deepest displeasure.

In some years we went with Mike's father Pat Patterson, who, it is said, appeared as a child in *Gone with the Wind*. It hardly seemed possible, since he was a towering figure of rough-hewn authority whose even larger station wagon was well suited for a collection of noisy young birders. His experiences as a Boy Scout leader also served him well in keeping a herd of sixteen-year-old ne'er-do-wells in line. The joy of these trips was little marred by "adult problems" such as flat tires or the terminal clank as the transmission arbitrarily terminated its heretofore blissful coitus with the engine and gearcase of Pat's wagon and fell to the ground. We did not have to solve those problems, we could just go birding or climb the butte and hold hands in the gathering dusk while nighthawks dove overhead calling "beernt!" Indeed, the phrase "looking for nighthawks" came to mean going off to hold hands in the dark.

I can recall no joy in birding greater than being at Malheur in those early years with my friends, not having to worry about anything more complicated than getting back to the dorm in time for dinner, or how to identify a Sage Thrasher. Some combination of teenage metabolism, relative freedom from care, the intrinsic glory of Malheur itself, and the nature of friendship combined to crystallize those years forever. My poem *Malheur at Fourteen* ends with the following stanza:

> *So I brought you today*
> *to show you the place*
> *that he thought was closest to heaven*
> *in the hope that someday*
> *you'll think of me here*
> *by the waters below the great mountain.*

It is hard to describe the effect of Malheur upon young people, except that it is glorious, and to be encouraged. Go there.

I mentioned earlier that I helped edit the enormous reference work *Birds of Oregon*, which came out in 2003. In a sense the final form of that book was shaped at Malheur, where I met my two co-editors. Matt Hunter was sixteen when we first met at Malheur headquarters. He had come over with a school group and fell rapidly into Hooked On Malheur mode. In fact he was so hooked that we returned two weeks later in Matt's little Honda.

The following day, June 8, 1980, we were at headquarters in the morning, Matt having re-digested the entire field guide the night before. As we looked up into the trees east of the main building, he said, "Isn't this a Chestnut-sided Warbler?" Well, of course it couldn't be, except that it was—Oregon's eighth record. That got our trip and our friendship off to a snappy start.

The following morning, June 9, we were in about the same place, floating along in the knowledge that we'd already found a fabulous bird for which we would be admired. Matt looked up into the tree— the same tree—and said, "Isn't this a Bay-breasted Warbler?" which of course it couldn't be, since there was only one previous Oregon record. Matt was overheating like many neophytes, seeing the Chestnut-sided again, poorly. Then the Bay-breasted came out into perfect view. Matt became a professional biologist and construction contractor and, with three young children, does not chase rarities much anymore, but I know he retains fond memories of those mornings.

One of the curious facts about my living and birding in a state with a fairly small population like Oregon is that I had been in the field for thirty-one years before ever meeting the dean of Oregon avian biologists, Dave Marshall, who had worked at Malheur in the 1950s. I owned his small book on birds of Northwest yards and gardens, and I had reprints of many of his articles, including the one he and friend Tom McAllister published in the *Auk*, North America's premier ornithological journal, when they were eighteen years old. Of course, he worked mainly with biologists, and was in Washington, D.C., during some of my most active years as a young rabble-rouser. I was, and am, a birder who writes, not a biologist.

It was therefore with great pleasure that I realized that the elfin man who emerged from Portland State University President Judith Ramaley's car at Frenchglen near the Malheur refuge in 1999 was Dave. He does not look anywhere near his age, even today at eighty-two, so it took a moment for recognition to soak in. In that moment of my weakness Dave somehow managed to combine in one slyly unpunctuated sentence:

"Great to meet you after all this time how would you like to help out in writing a new *Birds of Oregon*?"

If a respectable ornithologist ever asks you this kind of question, the best answer is "*No hablo Ingles, Señor*," followed by a careful withdrawal, never turning your back on the speaker. I said yes. Perhaps my most important contribution was introducing Dave to Matt. We had all started observing birds as teenagers, we met through our love for Malheur, and today the book is cited as Marshall, Hunter, and Contreras (2003).

Dave first went to Malheur in 1939, a two-and-a-half-day marathon just to *get* there from Portland over endless gravel and dirt roads, much like Dallas Lore Sharp described part of the journey in *Where Rolls the Oregon* (1914, reprinted in 2001 as *Eastern Naturalist in the West: Dallas Lore Sharp 1912*):

I had never ridden from Bend to Burns by auto-stage before, and I did not realize at first that you could hold yourself down by merely anchoring your feet under the rail and gripping everything in sight. It is a simple matter of using all your hands and knees and feet. But at the start I was wasting my strength, as, with eyes fixed and jaw set, I even held on to my breath in order to keep up with the car.

The desert was entirely new to me; so was the desert automobile. I had been looking forward eagerly to this first sight of the sage plains; but I had not expected the automobile, and could see nothing whatever of the sagebrush until I had learned to ride the car. I had ridden an automobile before; I had driven one, a staid and even-going Eastern car, which I had left at home in the stable.

I thought I knew an automobile; but I found that I had never been on one of the Western desert breed. The best bucker at the Pendleton Round-up is but a rocking-horse in comparison. I doubt if you could experience death in any part of the world more times for twenty dollars than by auto-stage from Bend to Burns.

The trail takes account of every possible bunch of sagebrush and greasewood to be met with on the way. It never goes over a bunch if it can go around a bunch; and as there is nothing but bunches all the way, the road is very devious. It turns, here and there, every four or five feet (perhaps the sagebrush clumps average five feet apart), and

it has a habit, too whenever it sees the homesteader's wire fences,
of dashing for them, down one side of the claim, then short about
the corner and down the other side of the claim, steering clear of all
the clumps of sage, but ripping along horribly near to the sizzling
barbs of the wire and the untrimmed stubs on the juniper posts; then
darting off into the brush, this way, that way, every way, which in
the end proves to be the way to Burns, but no one at the beginning
of the trip could believe it – no one from the East, I mean.

... It was 7:10 in the morning when we started from Bend, it was
after eight in the evening when we swung into Burns.

Dave's trip at age thirteen was a precursor or premonition: Dave became refuge biologist at Malheur in 1955-1960. I first went at fourteen in 1970 and Matt at sixteen in 1980. Such is the magnetism of this pilgrimage.

I missed a year or two of Malheur trips when I was in college (I did not learn to drive until I was twenty-six and inherited a car) and the three years I was in Missouri, but otherwise I have been to Malheur at least once a year, sometimes three or four times, for over thirty years. I have been there close to a hundred times. I will go there as long as I can. I will eventually go there permanently: my ashes will be scattered there, where I will join my birding friends Joe Evanich and Martha Sawyer forever.

Why? What is so special about Malheur that brings me back to the mosquitoes, the dust, the hard water and thunderstorms? The only possible answer is "everything."

First, of course, there are the birds. It is likely that more species of birds can be seen and heard from the front lawn of Malheur headquarters than from any other single location where an observer can stand in Oregon, perhaps in the whole northwestern quarter of North America. Every migrant passerine species crossing the Great Basin, with a few exceptions that use only specialized habitat, stops in the horseshoe of trees that shelters the headquarters complex. Even some of the supposedly specialized species stop in—for example the Canyon Wren that spent a day exploring the roof of the bunkhouse. Every waterbird, hawk, owl, and hummingbird that passes through eastern Oregon is probably visible at some time from that same lawn, by virtue of the fact that there is a large pond right below the lawn and the shores of the lake itself are visible by scope in the distance.

Only at a few places such as Malheur headquarters can the Northwest produce a movement of migrants reminiscent of the "waves" so prevalent in the eastern U.S. On one day in the late 1970s I walked into the headquarters complex to find a good swarm of migrants and took a minute to realize that the reason the hawthorn tree looked a little odd was that it contained forty-five male Western Tanagers. There were no females. There were no tanagers in adjacent trees. I do not know why. I have not seen that episode repeated, but there have been days when fifty flycatchers would suddenly appear overnight, or a surge of towhees, or nothing but vireos. Most often, a wide variety of species is present in smaller numbers.

In addition to the immense migratory flow of normal Northwestern species through headquarters, vagrants from elsewhere in North America are found here more often than in any other Northwest location. Such unlikely visitors as Worm-eating Warbler, Yellow-throated Vireo, and Streak-backed Oriole have appeared in these trees. Why?

The headquarters complex is an oasis in two kinds of desert, a rare situation that acts as a magnet for any bird passing through the region. It is an oasis of trees in a region dominated largely by sagebrush desert with a few alfalfa fields. It is also an oasis of land bordered on the north by what is, in some years, the largest lake in Oregon. Any bird crossing that lake from the north will see one large grove of trees on its shore and go there. Any bird starting to cross that lake from the south under adverse weather conditions may well change its mind and double back to the shelter of the grove.

But it is not just the rarities or the sheer volume of birds that makes this one spot so attractive to observers. It is the kind of experiences that an observer can have there. Over the years I have seen Great Horned, Barred, Barn, Northern Saw-whet and Flammulated Owl there, perfectly visible, perched in the trees during the day. Except for Barred I have seen each of these more than once.

One time we had been working our way around the trees finding nothing special when suddenly an extraordinary electrical rattling similar to that made by a rattlesnake went off in a small bush right ahead of us. I stuck my head through an intervening spruce branch and saw about eight Ruby-crowned Kinglets all ticking away at about twice their normal speed. They were all facing the same way, so I followed their look and realized that a Saw-whet Owl was sitting in the center of the little bush. Saw-whets are partially migratory and often occur on the refuge in October. This particular one stayed too long—its remains were found a couple of days later, apparently dinner for the resident Great Horned Owls.

But it is not all birds at headquarters. One day I was walking back from the museum area when an oddly shaped object bounced out of the grass and toward the trees. At first I could not tell what kind of mammal had a head the size of a football stuck on the body of a serpent. A couple of additional ineffectual hops made the situation clear: a young long-tailed weasel had caught a very large robin and was attempting to transport it somewhere for conversion into weasel.

The robin was dead by then, but was too large for the weasel to carry while walking or running in the usual manner of mustelids because it dragged on the ground. The weasel was therefore reduced to a peculiar kangaroo-like motion toward its goal: a surging forward leap got the robin clear of the ground, but the imbalanced load then brought the front of the weasel back to earth sooner than it expected based on past experience, resulting in an ignominious compressed plunge back to the earth. Nonetheless this immense galumphing inchworm managed to get across the path and into the shelter of the stone wall with its prize.

In the early 1990s a wet year brought all manner of snakes and other animals out of their usual holes and onto the roads. Along with them came a somewhat bemused bobcat, which wandered around the display pond at midday, apparently flooded out of some comfortable cave. It stared at the ducks on the pond from several angles, but getting at them was impractical so eventually it settled down to wait for some hapless vole to wander by. In 2004 a bobcat actually had its kittens under part of the headquarters deck complex.

In the fall, Lewis's Woodpeckers pass through the refuge in small numbers. On one occasion I observed one crawling carefully about in the apple tree near the museum. I say "crawling" because Lewis's Woodpeckers do not always act the way you'd expect a respectable woodpecker to behave. Indeed, this particular one was not pecking wood at all, the shame. It was eating apples. And it was very picky, or perhaps was bored easily. After hacking open an apple and taking a few bites, it would move on to another apple. Most astonishing of all, it had a shadow: a male Western Tanager followed it through the tree, finding apples that had been opened and then taking bites itself.

It appeared that the tanager preferred to let the woodpecker do the work of breaking through the apples' skin, then would nibble the opened fruit.

On a recent trip, one Lewis's mistook a birder for a tree. Steve Mlodinow, the brilliant and colorful regional editor for *North American Birds*, was standing near the stone wall at the west side of the main lawn when the woodpecker swooped slowly across the compound and latched onto the back strap of Steve's baseball cap. It looked around for a moment, then lurched off into the trees. It did not decide to check Steve's skull for grubs, which was something of a pity. Had it done so, a great deal of his personality might have been explained.

In the 1970s and '80s, Benson Pond was a popular lunch stop because it is about halfway down the valley between headquarters and Frenchglen, has good local birding, and has parking for several vehicles with a turnaround area. After high water damaged the bridge abutments in the late 1990s, the road into the parking area was closed to vehicles and anyone interesting in checking the area had to walk in. It is therefore somewhat less visited because of the quarter-mile walk in and out. However, the birds are still there waiting, as are the mosquitoes, for which Benson Pond is justly famed.

The walk in can be oppressive on a hot day, but invigorating when cooler. The road lies adjacent to the pond, on the south side of which a pair of Trumpeter Swans often breeds. This walk is a great place to get excellent looks at Marsh Wren, Common Yellowthroat, and the swallows that habitually roost on the half-dead tree by the bridge. Some astonishing birds have been found here over the years, including Summer Tanager, Northern Parula, Cape May Warbler, Mourning Warbler, Baltimore Oriole, and Chestnut-sided Warbler.

It also once harbored the most perfect fake among birds that I have ever found. In the late 1980s I was wandering around the small trees at the eastern end of the stand when I heard a Prairie Warbler song. At the time I had never seen a Prairie Warbler and I knew I was about to, so I summoned other birders. We carefully triangulated on the song and eventually encircled one fairly small Russian-olive tree.

A Russian-olive, although inherently wicked as an introduced species upon which Starlings in particular rely for food, is a great tree for birds and birders alike because of its structure. At first glance it appears willow-like, but more pale olive-green than the bright yellow-green of a willow. However, it is structurally different, having a somewhat more open character, with a bit less foliage. This means that it has enough cover for birds to use, but not enough to allow them to hide from a slavering horde of birders wanting to see, for example, a Prairie Warbler.

We therefore approached this particular Russian-olive with a certain swaggering confidence based on our abilities as birders combined with our knowledge that with several of us surrounding the tree, the bird would quickly be seen and could not fly out undetected. In fact, the bird was seen quite quickly indeed, and we could even watch its bright yellow throat as it sang. Unfortunately the rest of it was bright yellow too: it was manifestly a Yellow Warbler, of which none of us had seen fewer than seventy-five that morning, since Malheur is a major population center for the species.

We kept looking behind and around it for the Other Bird, the Prairie Warbler that must by definition be uttering the notes we heard every time the Yellow Warbler opened its bill. There were no other birds in the tree. The Yellow Warbler, which to make matters worse appeared visually to be a female, which should not sing at all, was busy cranking out a Prairie Warbler song, which sounds totally different in tone, cadence, and character from a Yellow Warbler song. At no time did it utter any sound that belonged to a Yellow Warbler. I don't know why it did this.

I was reminded of this bird years later under different circumstances when I attended the monthly "Birders' Night" news and picture meeting at the Portland Audubon Society center. Someone whose name I do not recall had brought a very good video, as he often did, but I don't think he had checked the sound before he brought it, or did not realize what was happening. His video was taken from below and in front of a perched Tree Swallow, which preened, gazed about, and sang; that is, it made the rich, chirpy notes that pass for song among swallows.

Somehow the videographer's sound pickup was not aimed directly at the swallow but below it somewhat, because every time the swallow opened its bill to burble, a rather loud Common Yellowthroat song was heard from the bushes below. About half the audience—those who knew the songs—started laughing. The other half looked around in quizzical inquiry. Just *what* were they missing?

Burrowing Owls. Ramiel Papish

Birders' Night produced some other humorous events, the most telling of which were the Shorebirds from Heck. There were two such events. One involved a birder who today serves on the Oregon Bird Records Committee. He had taken some shorebird photos at the coast and apparently had not checked them very closely. He had started showing his slides and describing a Sharp-tailed Sandpiper, when a couple of people in the darkened room started making strange barking noises: "ruff! ruff!" Which is what the bird was, an immature Ruff.

The other was a rather sorry affair in which a birder had traveled the length of the state to get photos of the state's first Wilson's Plover, but when he started showing the slides, they showed a golden-plover. Somehow he had latched onto the wrong bird at some point.

⮎

Returning to Malheur, it is worth noting that what makes Malheur such a special draw for birders is that it is one of those places that is, as a whole, far greater than the sum of its parts. The parts alone take days to observe and enjoy, and even then it is possible to visit only a portion of the refuge complex. For many Oregon birders, myself included, going to Malheur is both a birding experience and a sort of spiritual retreat.

One reason that the refuge has this special place in many birders' lives is that it is rather isolated, three hundred miles from Oregon's population centers, hemmed in on three sides by cliffs and hills, with the vast shield of Steens Mountain filling the sky to the southeast, providing part of the valley's water from snowmelt. Away from the northern part of the refuge, many cell phones reach nothing and a person who chooses to be alone in the desert or valley can do so most of the year.

The Malheur Field Station, a collection of old Job Corps buildings and Eisenhower-era house trailers dropped in 1964 apparently from the sky onto bare sage desert a few miles from refuge headquarters, has a couple of phones in the main buildings, but the rooms and trailers rented by guests have no connections to the outside world. There are no televisions, no phones, no radios. Anyone who brings any of these with them will find that there is not much reason to have done so. The station added wifi service in 2007; whether that is a virtue remains to be seen, but I am cautiously optimistic.

In the spring, staying at the field station brings a visitor face to face with nature in its most active state. Cliff and Barn Swallows nest right on the guest structures, and when you go outside you either flush them in all directions or, especially in the case of Cliff Swallows, they will sit in their clay-pot nests and gaze out at you with a suspicious, malignant stare. Say's Phoebes also nest on-site.

A May morning starts very early at the field station. Long before daylight—indeed, before there is any apparent light at all—swallows start zipping around the buildings calling loudly. They usually drown out the Sage Thrashers, which sometimes start singing earlier (if they bothered to stop at all during the night) but which are usually farther away. By the time most observers have staggered to breakfast and commented on how cold a May morning can be at four thousand feet, every other creature has stirred.

These mornings are even more spectacular in the marshes and at headquarters, where the sheer variety of sounds can be overwhelming as the singing imperative takes over and spring is declared for all comers to hear. Walking into the headquarters complex at dawn in late spring is one of the great anticipatory moments in an Oregon birder's life: What has arrived overnight? What strange and exciting song might herald a rare vagrant? And best of all, if you get there early enough when it is still chilly, most of the mosquitoes have not yet emerged from the grass.

Yet for some of us, Malheur in the fall has equal charms as a birding destination and a place for contemplation. For in the fall, if you go to the field station or any other reasonably isolated place, you will hear that rarest of sounds in our modern world: silence. An evening at the field station in late September, when most of the tourists have gone and only a few birders are around, can be a time of extraordinary beauty and quiet, when literally no sounds can be heard for many long minutes, even half an hour or more. There is just the sky, the sage, the backdrop of Steens Mountain and the occasional rabbit passing by.

The mountain, yes, there is nothing like it, in its own separate world. But it took me a few more years to discover that world.

1975: Childhood's End

Lake Mosquito

It was a long way up (the twenty-odd feet could have been a hundred) and the hole at the top looked very small indeed from inside the volcano. It is true that this particular volcano, Little Belknap Crater, had ceased producing lava in, oh, 880 B.C., but then the Cascade volcanoes are technically dormant, not extinct, and what was I doing inside one?

We who live near these beautiful snow peaks were reminded of their undead status recently with the announcement that the flank bulge on South Sister was growing at a rate of *an inch a year*—none of this centimeters per decade business, this volcano is bulging *right now*, almost fast enough to see. Geologists with a sense of humor say that well, the bulge *could* be caused by a lot of water building pressure in underground chambers. Oh, sure it is.

We left me inside Little Belknap, confirming my claustrophobia as the scout camp's program director Mike Adams and the others noticed my reluctance to enter the lava tubes inside the crater. These tubes spread from the sides of the crater floor, and get smaller as you go into them. Who in their right mind would go in there, I shuddered? Well, I was supposed to be leading gawky pods of Boy Scouts on that very hike and into this very crater starting the following week, during my summer as a camp ranger in the High Cascades of Lane County in 1975.

The others went out first, except for Mike, and with a certain amount of hauling on the very stout rope that we had belayed outside, I was dragged (honesty compels me to omit the word "climbed") out of the crater and crawled gratefully onto the surrounding pulverized lava. Yes, I would see the sun again. The trees were still there, and the passing Clark's Nutcrackers appeared to sense that anyone so abject as I, staggering to my feet after emerging from a direct route to fire and brimstone, was unlikely to have any food worth stealing.

Little Belknap is easily seen from the Dee Wright Observatory at the summit of tortuous McKenzie Pass. It is the deceptively delicate little summit shouldering above the lava fields to the northwest. In fact, most of the newest lava around the summit came from this amazingly small spigot. Tourists generally ignore it, looking instead at the vast snowy skirts of the Three Sisters right next door to the south of the highway, or the iconic spire of Mt. Washington and the more distant Fuji-cones of Jefferson and Hood to the north.

Visiting the High Cascades for a day as a tourist is different from living there for five weeks as I did as a camp ranger for Camp Melakwa in August 1975. A discreet conversation between the camp leaders led to my transfer from volcano-diver, a role for which I was clearly

Pileated Woodpeckers. Ramiel Papish

unsuited, to running the archery range, for which I was obviously more qualified by virtue of having never raised a bow in my life, therefore having never demonstrated my incompetence. I was a pretty good archery range person and a scout only shot at me once: I know John Christ didn't mean to do it; he was perfectly nice to me when I saw him fishing off the south jetty at Yaquina Bay a few years later. And where is that calm pescatore of the 1970s today, so many years later?

Melakwa is said by some to mean Big Mosquito in an Indian language, and no one who has worked there could argue that the mosquitoes, of whatever size, were uncommonly dedicated, abundant, fearless, and professional. One has to admire, from a certain distance, any job done well in nature, from the cross-ocean migration of hummingbirds to the capture of a sluggish goose by a Gyrfalcon. As a person interested in the natural world, I concede the mosquito its rightful place: biting someone else.

Melakwa Lake lies near Scott Lake just west of the North Sister and the Belknap flows. In the summer of 1975 the forest around the lake, a mix of true fir, mountain hemlock, and lodgepole pine, supported at least six American Three-toed Woodpeckers. It was hard to tell how many there really were, but one day between sessions at the archery range I walked the trail network and distinguished at least six birds that were in separate areas at the same time. This is an unusual concentration in an area that is not recently burned, and 1975 has proven to be an unusual year: other birders who have worked at the camp in subsequent years have found few or none.

Three-toed Woodpeckers have a rather quiet way of going about their business. They are mainly scalers, not hammerers, so instead of the heavy thumping of a Hairy Woodpecker or flicker on its favorite echo-snag, or the savage hacking of a Pileated in one of the larger trees, we had to listen for the more subtle tap-tap-tap of a Three-toe knocking loose slices of bark. We could tell where they had been by looking for recent pale vertical ovoid patches on the less robust-looking pines, and sometimes on the firs. These patches rarely look natural because they are not simply sloughed bark, which tends to come loose in more ragged patterns. They are typically surrounded, at least in part, by pretty solid-looking bark.

The Melakwa Lake area does not have a great variety of bird life because there is really only one habitat there, the mixed forest of the Cascade summit. It is therefore full of juncos, Gray and Steller's Jays, Mountain and sometimes Chestnut-backed Chickadees, the occasional kinglet or nuthatch, a rather sparse chorus of ventriloquial Hermit Thrushes, the odd flyover Vaux's Swift, Evening Grosbeak, or Pine Siskin, and not much else except an occasional Barrow's Goldeneye on the lake.

However, there are compensations for someone who spends time in the summit region. One day I was walking the trails with Mike Patterson when a pine marten suddenly ducked onto the path, classified us as Edible; Too Large, and ran off into the forest. That is the only marten I have ever seen. There are bats around the lake, and the evenings spent in the blufftop amphitheater on the west side of the lake offer a sight never visible from our cities at dusk: alpenglow on the Three Sisters, with superimposed bats.

The Sisters absorb half the eastern horizon from Melakwa Lake, but it is hard to see them because of the forest. The scout camp amphitheater provides a view over the top of the forest, and at dusk, with some fire smoke to discourage the mosquitoes, all of the land below is in darkness, but the mountains, their snow shields rising five thousand feet higher than the lake, catch the sun for another half-hour. The snow, the glimmering polished-pearl white snow of the daytime world, turns from molten peach to deep roseate in the quiet of the evening.

"When the gales of November come early"

I can't remember what time it was on the morning of November 9, 1975, but the pounding on the door of my one-room "apartment" at least *seemed* excessively early. I was in my first year at the University of Oregon, having graduated from South Eugene High School a year late owing to what I will call a bad attitude. Living largely off credit at Leslie's Mandarin Restaurant down the street, where the owners had known me since I was eleven, I was not having a good year, though by virtue of ignoring school I was able to find time to write a bit about birds.

The pounding continued, and when I opened the door I beheld the scarecrow figure of Tom Lund peering myopically down. Tom drove me crazy but he was one of the best birders in the state in those years, a Minnesotan who had come to Oregon by way of California.

Among other things he had found the state's first confirmed Buff-breasted Sandpiper and Bar-tailed Godwit, by looking exactly where they should have been. We, the rising stars of Oregon, had not been looking, and we learned a lot from Tom while he was here.

He was one of the least likely people to come to my door because there had always been a certain oil-and-water effect between us, yet there he was. He stared at me, then spoke as if under the influence:

"There are petrels and jaegers at Fern Ridge."

"Right. What time is it?

"There really are, I just came from there."

It was early in the morning and Fern Ridge Dam was half an hour away to the west, right at the eastern edge of the Coast Range. He must have been there at dawn. I had been vaguely aware of a storm coming in the night before, but I had seen storms in November since I could walk. He had paid closer attention to how strong that storm really was.

I went with Tom out to the dam. He mentioned that he had seen a couple of petrels and jaegers flying around in the gray dawn after he had stopped to check a bird hanging dead from a tangle of fishing line over the dam: a Leach's Storm-Petrel, he said. Right. The dam was fifty miles from the ocean, with the Coast Range in between. As we got to the dam, I could see an enormous swarm of birds over it. And hanging from the wire overhead in the clear morning light was a very dead Leach's Storm-Petrel, a bird that belonged over the open ocean.

Later that day the news reports came in and we began to understand what had happened. It was the worst windstorm since Columbus Day, 1962, but this time the winds had stayed more or less from the west, so we did not get the pea-shooter effect in the Willamette Valley as we had during the earlier storm. Instead, the southern Oregon coast was hammered. As the day went on, we heard that part of the roof of Marshfield High School in Coos Bay had blown off and that there had been enormous damage within an area about a hundred miles long. But just how strong had the winds been?

Word finally came out that the anemometer at the weather station at Cape Blanco, the windiest point on the coast, had gone to about ninety miles per hour early in the previous evening *and had stayed there for eight hours*, eventually recording long gusts to 130 mph before the entire apparatus was carried away. One report was of brief gusts to 145 mph. I have since been at Cape Blanco during recorded winds of sixty miles per hour, in which I was barely able to stand upright. What was a petrel or phalarope to do in winds of ninety-plus?

Die, for the most part. We went up on the dam and gazed at the mass of birds. Out over the lake we could see at least a dozen storm-petrels darting this way and that. I did not realize at the time that they are so adapted for salt water that they cannot drink fresh water for long and survive. They were also not finding much to eat on the lake. That morning we were eventually to witness an extraordinary commitment to science—or insanity—when Mark Nebeker, a birder who was my age, actually *swam out* from the dam into the cold storm-blown lake in order to recover a dead storm-petrel. Today he works for the Oregon Department of Fish and Wildlife near Portland and is never seen around Fern Ridge, no doubt permanently scarred by the experience.

Petrels were seen inland throughout southwestern Oregon. One observer was driving down Interstate 5 about sixty-five miles inland when a Leach's Storm-Petrel flew past his car. The farthest inland that we heard of was a bird picked alive from a snowbank above the town of Oakridge at three thousand feet. Its rescuer actually drove the bird all the way to the coast to release it, over one hundred miles west. It may have been the only survivor of the inland birds.

About forty dead storm-petrels were eventually recovered and sent off to the Museum of Vertebrate Zoology in California, where they proved to be of two subspecies. We had surreptitiously looked over a bag of them at a meeting of the Southern Willamette Ornithological Club, with Tom, George "Chip" Jobanek, and Don Payne showing us the differences. We all politely ignored the smell, which I was next to experience while transporting a Short-tailed Shearwater to a recovery center. Seabird oil is effective waterproofing, but it is made from what they eat. Enough said.

The birds blown in to Fern Ridge were not all petrels. Two tired but dangerous-looking Pomarine Jaegers sat quietly on the gravel as if daring us to approach closely. Out on the lake a flock of White-winged Scoters sailed along as though they belonged there, while a Whimbrel, rare inland in Oregon, limped along the nearby mud. But the most astonishing sight was over the front of the dam, for that is where the gulls had gathered.

There was no way to count them, but our best estimate by the morning's end was eight hundred Bonaparte's Gulls (twenty would have been normal), eight Black-legged Kittiwakes (the first we had ever seen inland), and at least one gorgeous Sabine's Gull, which I had seen before only while chumming my breakfast into the ocean from a boat.

Why I'm not chummy with pelagic birds

The first time I saw a Leach's Storm-Petrel it was in a very convenient place for me, flapping back and forth over the whitecaps of Fern Ridge Reservoir. That's where it needed to be for me, because the true bounding main is altogether too vigorous for my taste. I have done my time out on the heaving billows, and for that matter, my share of heaving into the billows. I have seen most of what there is to see out there, and plan to do the rest of my pelagic birding from locations no more unstable than, say, a jetty.

I admit that my pelagic trips were rewarding. The glorious sight of my first adult Sabine's Gull off northern California, seen through glasses smeared with scum from the huge wave that had just plastered the observers. The excitement of a nearby flock of albatrosses examining with interest the green hat that only moments before had protected my head from the thirty-knot breeze.

One time a Winter Wren popped aboard, apparently to dine on remnants of my breakfast that dotted the rail. One Oregon birder will doubtless remember the time I didn't make it to the rail. Well, he should have known better than to wear Guccis on a pelagic trip. Enough about the ugly past.

I recommend Solid Ground Pelagic Birding. There is a lot to be seen from the comfort of your neighborhood jetty or dike. I have seen the following in Oregon while standing on the ground: Northern Fulmar (lots, most years), Pink-footed Shearwater (many times), Sooty Shearwater (lots), Short-tailed Shearwater (lots), Fork-tailed Storm-Petrel (twice), Leach's Storm-Petrel (three times), Pomarine Jaeger (three times), Parasitic Jaeger (maybe fifteen times), Long-tailed Jaeger (three times), South Polar Skua (twice), Black-legged Kittiwake (zillions), Sabine's Gull (maybe a dozen times), Arctic Tern (lots; far fewer in the past fifteen years), and Cassin's Auklet (maybe a dozen times).As well as a frigatebird disturbing the gulls in the Charleston boat basin.

So the opportunities for land-based pelagic birding are substantial. Some points to remember for the birder whose innards churn at the mention of the word "gangplank": Pelagic birds show up in weird places where you don't even have to smell that special ocean aroma. Try Malheur or the eastern Oregon lakes in the fall for jaegers. They in particular can appear anywhere in the fall. All three have appeared at Fern Ridge Reservoir, fifty miles from the ocean in central Lane County. I once saw a Parasitic at Davis Lake in the central Cascades, eventually soaring out of sight above the lake, which lies at forty-five hundred feet. Parasitics have even been seen following tractors in the Willamette Valley. A Long-tailed Jaeger showed up at Haystack Reservoir in eastern Oregon one summer.

Sabine's Gulls pop up at inland lakes, too, especially in the fall. Big storms in the fall can splatter Leach's Storm-Petrels and other pelagic species inland as far as the Cascades, so check your local lakes after such rough weather.

At the coast, pick places where you are either sticking out into the ocean, e.g., jetties or headlands, or places where there is deep water near shore. Boiler Bay, Oregon, is one such place; check with local birders to find others. Most inland birders tend to go to the coast when the weather is really nice. For pelagics, try to go when it's nasty, particularly at the tail end of a storm with lots of wind. Some species are fairly easy to find at certain times of year along the Oregon coast, e.g., Northern Fulmars in late October and early November. Others appear when their food source is close to shore, e.g., shearwaters.

One technique for spotting pelagics is to watch incoming fishing fleets as they enter your range of vision; they often have a few shearwaters or kittiwakes hanging around. Always check big swarms of gulls; pelagics are often attracted to gull flocks. The same is true of flocks of diving pelicans. I have also had good luck with shearwaters in the summer when there are heavy fog banks offshore and clear weather right along the coast. They sometimes feed close to the beach under such conditions.

And go out on boats if you must. Give my regards to the birds I will doubtless not see often from land.

1976: The First Big Day

Why? Why try to find as many birds as possible in one day? Well, because we are birders and it is a challenge. Actually, I can't remember why we decided in May 1976, to try to break the two-week-old record of 142 species seen in one day in Oregon (on a Portland-to-Tillamook run), except that, well, *we* knew that *we* could find more because, well, *we* were the greatest.

That our big day was a last-minute decision can be seen in the date we went: May 28. As modern Big Day perpetrators know, this is two weeks later than the optimum mid-May time slot. However, we were taking our usual Memorial Day weekend trip to Malheur, and decided to reconfigure the trip to the refuge into a Big Day.

So who were we? In addition to me, the team consisted of Sayre Greenfield, Mike Patterson, and George "Chip" Jobanek. Chip and I were students at the University of Oregon (I had not yet been kicked out for nonperformance), Mike was at Oregon State, and Sayre was just home from his second year at Cornell.

We knew we were ending up at Malheur, but we needed to decide where to start. It had to be on the coast, and nearby Florence would not do because it has no rocks, therefore there would be no Black Oystercatchers. We knew we'd probably be too late for Black Turnstone and Surfbird, but if there were any stragglers, they would also be on the rocks.

Eventually we settled on Yachats, a small town about twenty miles north of Florence, because it has good visible rocks and a small creek mouth where late shorebirds might rest. Also, Oregon's one accessible colony of Rhinoceros Auklets lies between Yachats and Florence at Sea Lion Caves. Since we'd come back inland via Florence, we could pick up rhinos *en passant* rather than searching for them over the ocean somewhere else and probably missing them.

We waited at my house in Eugene for Mike Patterson, whom my mother went to collect at the bus station when he came in from Corvallis, then we left for the coast. Our oddest sight of that pre-count day was the female Rufous Hummingbird that had managed to get into the Safeway supermarket in Florence and was flying about in the upper part of the store. Whenever it landed on top of a light fixture a little puff of dust would appear, so we knew where it was (and how often Safeway cleaned the top of their fixtures).

We stayed the night in Florence, got up at 3:15 a.m., grabbed some foodlike objects and started up the coast. Our first bird was one we never saw: a night migrant Swainson's Thrush calling overhead as we left for Yachats. Yachats itself offered the predawn chatter of Violet-green Swallows shortly after 4:00 a.m.; they start feeding when they can't possibly see much. Can they?

We started back south to Florence when it was light enough to see. Tufted Puffins could still be found then at Heceta Head, though they are rare there today, perhaps owing to soil erosion. We did manage oystercatcher and a late Whimbrel, and also found Mountain Quail and Pileated Woodpecker, both missable, when passing through the Coast Range east of Florence later in the morning.

We were back in Eugene at 10:30 a.m., where we visited a known roosting Western Screech-Owl at the University of Oregon. We had not planned pre-dawn owling for this route. We also managed Burrowing, Great Horned, and Short-eared Owl, the latter two at Malheur.

In the evening at Malheur, we finished the day at a place that no longer exists, the so-called "Short Dike" road that led to Benson Boat Landing just northeast of the headquarters complex. That site, in the edge of Malheur Lake proper, provided access to the part of the refuge where White-faced Ibis, a rare bird at Malheur then, could sometimes be found. That proved to be our last bird of the day. Both the Benson Boat Landing area and the road were destroyed in the high water years of the 1980s.

At the end of the day we had driven 449 miles and found 157 species, a total that is by today's standards nothing special, but was a state record at the time. Chip got all 157, I had 155, Mike and Sayre 154.

I ran a similar route again in a subsequent year with far more planning. We ran into a lot of bonus birds that day before the starter on Greg Gillson's car came apart during a foray to Big Lake and Hoodoo Butte in the High Cascades. We were delayed three hours by towing and replacement, and *still* made it to Malheur before dark and finished with 188 species (my own tally; I am not sure what the others had). Had we not had a breakdown, we would probably have broken two hundred that day, which has since been done on the Malheur run and the coast-to-Summer Lake route.

Finding that many birds in a day is not an "outdoorsy" experience or even a normal birding experience; it is perhaps the epitome of what one ornithologist called "bird golf." Nonetheless, it was a lot of fun and the beginning of some good weekends at Malheur.

1985: Steens Mountain

*"... As wonder alternates
with thunderstruck, we fail the tourist test.
Our camera keeps its cover on as scrolls
unroll behind our eyes, where clever scribes
immersed in metaphor and metered verse
relate in great detail what we behold."*

David Hedges, "Steens Mountain Sunrise"

Mother of waters and father of storms. That is how my own poem entitled "Steens Mountain" begins. It is those things, but, from a distance, the mountain as seen from the west does not seem that impressive. Sure, there is snow on it most of the year, but then the valley floor below it lies at four thousand feet, so snow does not seem like that big a deal. And it has an interesting craggy skyline. So what's the excitement?

For someone who never leaves the Blitzen Valley during a visit to Malheur, Steens Mountain can appear to be simply a backdrop, more interesting than sky but basically just painted onto the cloud-flow. You can read in refuge literature that the mountain provides a lot of the water that allows the refuge to live, yet this is simply another fact among many facts. It is the sheer scale of the mountain, combined with its origin, that allow it to stay in the background for those who do not consider it worth a closer look.

First of all, it does not look like any of Oregon's other high mountains. The higher Cascade peaks are classic volcanic cones that cumulate in a defined point and rise majestically (or at least distinctively in the case of extrusive Mt. Washington and indicative Three-fingered Jack) over the surrounding terrain. The Wallowas are not volcanic but they, too, have in significant measure the properties of loftiness and grandeur that we expect of mountains. Steens Mountain does not look like this—at first.

Fault blocks such as Steens arise as a result of tectonic pressures, and there is some variation in how they look. Steens Mountain is a classic fault block and a large one. Its basic formation extends more than fifty miles in a rough north-south direction. From the west—the direction from which most people see it—the mountain's size is not readily apparent, due in part to the gradualness of its rise and in part to the way most people travel in the valley: much of it is simply not visible owing to intervening cliffs or the way its northern end curves to the east. Yet its summit ridge lies at an elevation over nine thousand feet and the highest point just under ten thousand feet.

It is from the east that the sheer mass of the mountain is most apparent. Seen from the Alvord Desert, from Highway 95 or the Whitehorse Ranch road, it is by far the most dominant feature of the landscape, rising five thousand feet almost sheer from the floor of the Alvord and extending unbroken to the north and south, a primal wall that makes of the Blitzen Valley a riparian garden and of much of southeastern Oregon a drier desert, where kit fox, leopard lizard, cacti, Black-throated Sparrows, and other species more common in the southern Great Basin can be found. There are even indigenous fish here, trout and the Borax Lake chub.

Yet even this view does not give you the true mountain, the uniqueness of its towering presence over all of southeastern Oregon. To know the mountain you must go upon it.

The road up Steens Mountain is usually open from late June through October, depending on snow levels. Its lower section does not immediately impress the observer: instead of a flat expanse of sagebrush, there is a sloping expanse of sagebrush. Sometimes Sage Grouse can be seen here. Soon a dense juniper forest clothes the view. In fall, these stands are an important food source for migrant Townsend's Solitaires and robins, which eat the berries.

The slope is easy but the climb is steady, and after a couple of miles in the juniper stands, the expanse of the upper mountain is suddenly closer, its massive shoulders partly hidden behind bluffs as the road winds through several small basins. The first stands of aspen appear above the juniper zone, strung along where there is a little more water: at the base of low rounded hills, in creek bottoms, around grassy sinks. After a while the sheer *volume* of aspen on the mountain becomes apparent: great sheets called clones because of their shared

root system ripple on the hillsides, endless fingers probe every distant
rivulet and cranny. And still the massif rises and spreads to the horizon
north and south.

Fish Lake campground just below the upper snow gate and Jackman
Park just above the gate provide an opportunity to explore the interior
of these aspen clones. I always think of these places as sapsucker
havens. Both Red-naped and *daggettii* Red-breasted Sapsucker occur
here, the latter rarely. Like most vegetative monocultures, aspen clones
do not offer much species variety, but the stands on Steens Mountain
provide a good opportunity to get to know sapsuckers, as well as
other common breeders such as House Wrens. There are said to be a
few pairs of Goshawks breeding on the mountain, though I have only
seen them here as a rare fall migrant.

These vast aspen carpets are also home to a very rare Oregon
mammal, the wolverine. The lower parts of the mountain sometimes
offer good looks at pronghorn (also known as antelope), while mule
deer are fairly common up to timberline where cattle are not grazing.
Above these lake basins as the trees thin and give way to grass and
sagebrush, the number of breeding species, avian, mammalian and
everything else, is quite low owing to the limited habitat. Yet it is just
here, as the "habitat" seems to be disappearing and the dominance of
sheer stone becomes overwhelming, that Steens Mountain offers its
greatest wonders to an observer.

In late summer and early fall, these grassy, stony ridges offer a look
at a phenomenon not easily observed in the western states' heavily
forested mountains: the southward migration of hummingbirds and
of hawks. Although the raptor movement is rather spread out, it can
be obvious on warm days, when several species pass long the upper
western slopes of the mountain and the exposed ridgeline. Red-tailed
Hawks, accipiters, and falcons are usually the most obvious migrants
here, but in some years a small, early movement of Rough-legs is
apparent. Northern Harriers sometimes move along the slopes in
customary harrier fashion, but can also startle an unprepared observer
by moving rapidly along the ridgetop like bulky falcons.

Even less visible to most observers is the southbound movement of
hummingbirds. In late summer, these alpine grasslands are often the
only places that still have recent flowers upon which hummingbirds
can feed. Western hummingbirds have a somewhat circular migration
route in latitude, longitude, and altitude. For example, Rufous

Hummingbirds move north in February and March mainly through lowland western Oregon, entering higher-elevation areas of eastern Oregon later in spring. By June, males have departed their breeding grounds and are moving upslope—some are even moving southward this soon. By late summer many hummingbirds are moving southward along the flowering ridgetops, and many of them use the upper slopes of Steens Mountain.

On one occasion in late August 1985, I was sitting on a rock near the head of Kiger Gorge, having carefully avoided seeing the Black Rosy-Finches I had come to see. Below me, the near-vertical headwall of this classic glacial gorge plunged downward until it sloped out into the edges of an aspen grove that seemed tiny so far below. There was a break in the wall to my left, and the availability of seeping water had allowed a growth of low shrubs and forbs to run almost vertically up the last fifty feet of headwall and over onto the plateau.

My attention kept wandering over to these low plants because I kept thinking that I saw birds there, yet I could never find anything. Finally I realized that hummingbirds were appearing in a steady stream at the low end of the fissure and feeding their way up to the top, after which they flew off to the south over the plateau. These were mostly Rufous, but there was at least one Calliope. On the other side of the plateau a year later I saw a Broad-tailed Hummingbird, a very elusive bird in Oregon, not—quite—proven to breed but it certainly does in good years.

As far as I could tell, these hummers had worked their way either up Kiger Gorge along the bottom or, perhaps more likely, along its sides where there were late flowers blooming. As they reached the headwall they were funneled toward the fissure across from me, which served as an upward chute to channel them out of the gorge in the right direction.

Sitting on the rocks at the head of Kiger Gorge is something I do not do very often. There is just you and the gorge:

The edge of awe awaits
watchers on the cliff
there is no rail
just the air
below us
forever.

Kiger Gorge itself is perhaps the greatest visual wonder on the mountain. Completely invisible from the west unless you realize what lies below the mountain's northwestern rim, it is a glacially scooped valley with a creek and aspen along the bottom, but from the overlook at its head, the aspen and everything else below has a toylike, miniaturized quality because it is fifteen hundred feet below at the headwall and extends into the far distance before curving slightly to the west. If there are no tourists around, you can hear a low purr from the gorge, the distant sound of the creek and the wind in the aspen, with the occasional croak of a raven drifting across the canyon.

It was here at the head of Kiger Gorge that I eventually saw my first Black Rosy-Finch. A few pairs nest here, as they do elsewhere along the rocky ridges. Adapted for the harsh realities of life in a world of ice, snow, and rock, they nest in holes in the cliffs, females choosing from among the much commoner males. Because of the sparse pickings in alpine grasslands, they cover large distances to feed, even in the breeding season. In fall, large flocks form, moving along the cliff faces and remnant snowfields like leaves tossed by the wind.

Rosy-finches are generally unwary if they happen to come near you. In general you can't approach them simply because they are one hundred feet straight down on a talus slope covered with snow, but if they come up the ridgeline they can sometimes be seen quite well. On one occasion I was resting on the edge of the cliff about half a mile northwest of the East Rim overlook, unhappy that the finches were not around, when suddenly they *were* around, sweeping around a stone pillar, chirping richly, and landing almost on top of me. In fact they started coming directly toward me on the ground so quickly that I had to scramble backward with my camera to keep them in focus—they were too close.

As you approach the East Rim the world suddenly ends not where you think it will—on the east—but on the west, where the headwalls of Big Indian Gorge and the Little Blitzen suddenly dive into its chasm, revealing another extraordinary aspen-lined canyon extending endlessly to the west. Do not think too carefully about what this means, because in fact you are driving along what amounts to a hogback ridge of rock a hundred yards wide that drops off about two thousand feet on the west and five thousand feet on the east.

The East Rim provides the best eastward view from the mountain. The Alvord Desert stretches dimly into infinity while a scattering of ranches seem right next door, after a fashion. Sure, they are five thousand feet more or less straight down, but the air is usually so clear that they are as crisp as though you could walk over and say hello. The actual summit of the mountain, a couple of miles to the south, is something of an anticlimax because it has only a small parking area, is often stuffed with tourists, and the trail to the rocky top leads mainly to a cluster of transmission towers. However, there is an interesting little cirque just below the parking area that sometimes has finches, siskins, pipits, or other birds. Any of the rocky ridges along the mountain might have bighorn sheep as an added bonus to the birding and extraordinary visual images of the mountain itself.

1986-1991: The Mountains of Home

From Steens Mountain there are few outdoor experiences in the Northwest that would not seem like a letdown. Among those that stand comparison are Mt. Rainier, the Wallowas, and the all but incomprehensible statement that is Crater Lake.

Crater Lake today retains much of the sense of mystery that it had for Indian tribes, early European explorers, and nature writers such as Walter Prichard Eaton and Roger Tory Peterson. Anyone who reaches the rim today and looks down (so far down) and across (can it really be so far across?) can't help but think of the sheer length of geologic time, the immeasurable power of natural forces, and the good fortune of those who are able to experience the result.

There is a strangely "unnatural" sensation when viewing this entirely natural lake, perhaps because it has such an unusual color, is typically still and empty when viewed by tourists, and is so unlike other montane sites. Awe is an overused word and concept, yet it is the best word for most people who see the lake for the first time.

Eaton's description provides a sense of what a newcomer finds at the rim:

Stopping the car beside the hotel, we still could see no lake, for in front of us was that rise of gray ash, like a sand-bar, cutting between us and the sky. Springing out over the doors and laden running-boards, we dashed up this slope—and stopped abruptly.

Directly under our feet the earth fell away in a vast slide of rock and volcanic ash, at an angle of at least fifty degrees. It fell away for eleven hundred feet, and if you once started down the incline, you would keep on to the bottom. It fell away into a huge hole, and as we looked to right and left, and then across, we saw this hole as an almost perfect circle, six miles in diameter. At the bottom of the hole lay Crater Lake, with the evening stillness coming on it, so that it held in reflection all the slides and snowdrifts and white-capped lava pinnacles that ring it round, held them reflected in a mirror of inconceivable blue.

You have seen water blue as the sky, but this is not sky-blue, it is much deeper and richer. It is not Mediterranean nor Caribbean blue. It is a strange, opalescent indigo, with a penumbra of green around the margin where there are shallows. It is opalescent indigo – and yet that does not describe it, for it is capable of many variations and mystic changes, dusky moods of Prussian grayness, richer moments, under a wild sunset, of solemn purple; yet always somehow, itself, its own incomparable and indescribable color.

From *Skyline Camps*, Walter Prichard Eaton, 1922, p. 133-34

Against the backdrop of this most unusual montane feature in Oregon, the birdlife can seem not only limited but somewhat comical, lacking in the dignity that we might expect in our anthropomorphic branding of wildlife occurring in such a place. The reason for this is fairly simple: birds land on people here. In particular, Gray Jays and Clark's Nutcrackers all but shove people out of the way in order to get at anything that looks like a handout in the main parking area. Tourists have been feeding the birds and squirrels here for generations, so that one might almost expect new subspecies to have developed: Gray Popcorn-Jay (*Perisoreus canadensis maizeophila*) and Clark's Cornnutcracker (*Nucifraga columbiana snacclepticus*).

It is all very well to have the well-known camp robber make an attempt on your sandwich or peanut-sack as you stand by the car. This behavior is, if you will, within the rules of engagement for humans and Gray Jays in semi-wild settings. It may be disconcerting to see half your lunch go lurching off between the pines dangling from the bill of a Gray Jay, but anyone with any experience in the outdoors must concede that the jay is playing fair and has behaved in a professional manner.

It is quite another experience to have barely emerged from your car, innocent of food and unaware that you have made a crunching sound with a sack, then to turn around and see the dagger-tipped bulk of a full-bodied nutcracker—no mere jay but a small crow in fact—coming full-throttle in a power dive from the nearest tree straight for your head—and landing on it. Sometimes they land on your outstretched hand, which is a far different experience from the reasonably delicate in-and-out of a Gray Jay. The descending whump of a nutcracker requires some preparation.

Eaton noted another phenomenon of the isolated rocky points in and around the lake:

And as if further to remind us of this power of hers, which is the secret of her magic, the bird life of the Phantom Ship, invisible from afar, was disclosed to us as we explored, entranced, the southern rock face – disclosed by a buzzing hum over our heads. Looking up, incredulous, we saw not one humming-bird, but no less than a score, hovering over the pentstemon [sic] and paintbrush, their tiny wings beating to a blur as they hung suspended against the face of the cliff, or carrying them with darting flight from rock to rock. One expects to see nothing less than a bald eagle on the crags of Crater Lake – and here, in the very heart of the frozen upheaval, were the darting wings of humming-birds, the thrust of dainty bills into the honey drop of a flower!

Skyline Camps, p. 155-56

There are birds at Crater Lake in addition to the thieves of the parking and picnic areas. The Rufous Hummingbirds noted by Eaton in the 1920s are still present, as are occasional other species such as Calliope, Black-chinned, and perhaps Broad-tailed, which has occurred nearby at Chemult and in the northern Rogue Valley. It is quite rare that far west.

Not until flowers are available in early May do hummers reach the Cascade summit ridges and Crater Lake. Male Rufous Hummingbirds excel at argument: they can be found in vigorous territorial disputes early in the breeding season (and at feeders any time). However, you need to watch them argue before midsummer: unlike many birds, male Rufous do not linger to enjoy the boreal summer, they buzz in, fight with each other, copulate, and buzz out, leaving females to do the difficult work in life, in much the same way that Congress relates to the operations of the federal government.

Unlike Congress, male Rufous hummers begin leaving in June, primarily by montane routes where flowers have just begun blooming. Thus some of Oregon's male Rufous may move south to wintering grounds in Mexico via the mountains of far eastern Oregon, or even the Rockies. For this reason, visitors to Crater Lake early in the season may well see plenty of males squabbling over penstemons, while people going after late June will see mainly females and young of the year, just as on Steens Mountain.

Birds of home

The streams falling away in all directions from the flattened hump of the Crater Lake massif are home to one of the two birds I missed most during the three years (1988-1991) that I lived in Missouri. They were as plain gray as a bird can be: the boulder-gray American Dipper (or water ouzel) and the mouse-gray Bushtit, which resembles nothing so much as a dust bunny with a tail stuck in rather unprofessionally on one end.

Of these, the dipper is the most distinctive, as it lives along, on, and in effect under montane streams. I have seen dippers disappear into shaded areas simply by sitting still, and I have seen them reappear simply by moving. The bird artist Lee Jaques once commented to his wife, after a frustrating day in the woods, that the difference between warblers and no warblers is very slight. The difference between a dipper and a wet lumpy stone in a river is very slight, too.

The early ornithologist Florence Merriam Bailey wrote of dippers that she saw in the Cascade Range:

When the ouzel started to swim, it would put its head under the water as if locating something, and then, quivering its wings, disappear altogether, coming up soon after with a long, black-shelled caddice fly larva, the shell of which, as we proved later, is a remarkable mosaic of minute stones ... when the bird brought up a grampus (as the larva is known locally), it would shake the long shell till it finally broke open, and, pulling out the yellowish brown larva, quickly swallow it.

After bringing up and eating several of the larvae, the ouzel picked about in the submerged green mats that suggested sea-weed.

Once it stood on a stone green with moss long enough to bring out the strong color contrast of the green and the gray. When walking about over the rocks it would make its droll little courtesies—dip, dip, dip—till you were constrained to speak its name—dipper.

When it had had a satisfying meal it flew across the river to a stone on the shaded bank, where, in terms of protective coloration, it perfectly pictured its background, for its gray upper parts disappeared in the dark shadow, the lighter shade of its breast toned in with the sun on the rock, and only its light-colored legs were left as slender sticks quite foreign to any bird-like suggestion. But when its profiled bill and head projected into the sun, the bird form was restored.

Florence Merriam Bailey, from *No Woman Tenderfoot: Florence Merriam Bailey, Pioneer Naturalist*, Harriet Kofalk, 1989, p. 138-41

I have no doubt that dippers wait for us to become accustomed to this up-and-down, in-and-out, and it is at that moment, when we gullible mammals are awaiting with confidence in our superior perception the reappearance of an ouzel from behind a rock, that the bird emerges directly out of the water twenty yards downstream, popping to a boulder top, bobbing briefly. The message is unmistakable: *You are in my realm, land-creature. Do not presume.*

Dippers are so at home in their element that they consider people simply additional impedimenta. When I was a kid birder, one of the older birders, Ina Foss, who had been around since Oregon was young and, according to local legend, had birded in Texas and Mexico with noted naturalist Luther Goldman, described sitting on the rocky edge of the McKenzie River and having a dipper pop up next to her, walk unconcerned across her dress-covered legs, and continue downstream.

At some locations on the Oregon coast where tumbling streams come all the way to the beaches, dippers can be found working their way into the edges of salt water. They are apparently able to eat a wide variety of small marine animals without respect to their seasoning.

Bushtits are a kind of seasoning, really. In an empty winter park on a chilly day they come boiling along like an avian pepper-storm, constantly relocating themselves with a distinctive *pst* note that sounds like they are spitting out a spider of which they didn't like the taste.

Bushtits have nested for many years on the Oregon State Capitol grounds. When I worked as a lobbyist in the 1990s I would always enter The Building (that is what lobbyists call the Capitol) by the east entrance in order to check on the status of the Bushtit nest in the large willow tree there. They were a constant reminder that what goes on inside The Building is, ultimately, of little consequence relative to what goes on in the willow tree.

In candor, Bushtits are not among the cleverest birds. One can ask only so much from a brain small enough to fit inside a Bushtit skull. Thus I was not completely surprised when a flock of them gathered around and tried to feed on a suet bar that I had just removed from the freezer and put outside on a very cold day. Those that merely hacked at it ineffectually suffered no harm, but one decided that it could really get something out of a particular crack and jammed its bill in.

The others flew off *pst*-ing in frustration while the enthusiastic bird, bill wedged in rock-hard suet, could not generate enough reverse energy with its miniature wings to back out, hovering momentarily as though to make itself a permanent attachment. It eventually remembered that it had legs (and an unimpressive set they are) and was able to get enough purchase to wrench itself out of the suet cake.

At any time of year, Bushtits are around to uplift our spirits by demonstrating that yes, there is fun to be had in the world.

Visions of home

Returning from my three years in Missouri, imagining these plain gray birds and the mountains and valleys that shelter them, I drove across the continent by way of Idaho. Having lived in far eastern Oregon as a teenager, I think of the sugar beet fields and sage flats as "home" in the same way as I view the forests and valleys of western Oregon. It was therefore no surprise that as the Snake River bridge came in sight along I-84, I felt a sense of having taken a very long parachute dive, about to end with my feet touching friendly soil at last.

I was not prepared, though, when, just as I reached the bridge, the radio started playing "Singing in the Rain."

For anyone traveling west across the desert of southeastern Oregon as I have done over a hundred times, there is no sight quite so imposing as that which greets a traveler cresting the rise two miles east of Brothers. Suddenly, as if placed there by Odin to guard the entrance to a sacred kingdom, the Three Sisters appear entire, distant yet, but bespeaking power held in check, strength far beyond what mere humans can construct.

The escorting spires and pinnacles of Bachelor, Broken Top, Washington, and Three-fingered Jack are not yet a major presence on the stage of nature, not at seventy miles distance, but the shield of the Cascade crest, raised against winter cold and western storms alike, never fails to speak to a stranger: "this far, and no further," while to a native the fingers of juniper, pine, and then fir beckon and signal "this way, this is the way to home."

[T]he Cascade Range, seen from the sage brush of eastern Oregon, is something totally different. It has a beauty and a haunting mystery all its own, that have remained unsung no doubt because so few travelers have had the chance to feel them. ...

Ahead of us stretched mile after mile of rolling sage brush, till the far-off, hazy forest began, rising in green waves of timbered foothill buttes to break at last against the blue rampart of the range. And rising from this range, remote, mysterious, dazzling, icy-white and beautiful, from Diamond Peak to the southwest clear to Jefferson in the north, stood the sentinel summits—the Three Sisters, Broken Top, Washington, Three Fingered Jack, with old Jefferson himself the highest, the most remote, the most inaccessible and alluring. He might have been a pyramid of glistening cloud.

These peaked white volcanoes, shooting up so far above the level of the blue range, seem to hold mystic converse one with another over the canyons between. Here in the desert, forty miles away from the nearest of them, their lower ledges were indistinguishable; they were solid cones of white. Indistinguishable, too, were the separate lower peaks around them. They but towered the crest of an unbroken wall.

...There is no mystic abyss as you approach the Rocky Mountains over the prairies. But here we found it, and those great dazzling cones which aspired so sublimely into the western sky, with the low sun dropping down to kindle their summits, were as cool, as aloof, as charged with mystery and portent, as the white gods of a dream.

Skyline Camps, Walter Prichard Eaton, 1922, p. 229-31

Jefferson Park

"Uphill? How far uphill? Carrying *what*?" Yes, well, it's possible that I once mentioned the idea, just as a concept, mind you, and as much as I'd like to see a Boreal Owl—that is, my commitment to advancement of science is strong, very strong indeed—but did you say *seven miles*?

Back home in Oregon after three years in Missouri, I felt that I should make some useful contribution to Oregon ornithology to offset the years of absence. I can't remember exactly how I ended up face-to-face with the Cascade Range in toto, the trailhead a dim, gaping hole in the trees, quite possibly filled with cougars and, even worse, spiders. Nonetheless, I had on my backpack, sleeping bag, and a curious elongated object of obscure function that resembled one leg of a small rhinoceros. The latter was in fact a leg, one-half of an ancient pair of pants, sewn shut across the bottom, with a belt slung through the original loops and over my shoulder. From its open upper end where one of my legs once went protruded a cluster of long aluminum poles. They were net poles, for we were going bird-banding. Seven miles uphill.

The Boreal Owl has a long history in Oregon, but the gap between the beginning of that history and its present status filled the better part of a century. In 1902, a dead Boreal Owl was found near Fort Klamath. For decades this was viewed as a freak event, an "accidental" occurrence in the words of my 1967 Peterson guide. The discovery of resident Boreal Owls in Colorado and Montana in the 1980s led investigators to look for them in Oregon, and to the astonishment of those of us who thought we knew the state's birds, Oregon was found to contain a small but widespread population of Boreal Owls. They occur in the Blue and Wallowa mountains and locally in the northern Cascade range. Their status in the Cascades was (and is) poorly known, so Mike Patterson and I decided in 1992 that what we needed to do was to go to some likely habitat and set up mist nets at night to catch a few, thereby advancing knowledge.

As it turned out, one of the most attractive and least-explored pieces of habitat we found was the Jefferson Park area within the Mt. Jefferson Wilderness about seventy-five miles east of Salem, Oregon. The area was open parkland with extensive meadows and clusters of Engelmann spruce and subalpine fir at about six thousand feet elevation just below the northern slope of Mt. Jefferson. This is theoretically perfect habitat for Boreal Owls.

I am a firm believer in the virtues of exercise; I just don't act on those beliefs very often. Thus I was not fully prepared for what it means to make the total transition from desk-jockey to Walter Prichard Eaton overnight. Yet Mike was heading up the trail with an obvious expectation that I would follow him, and Ram Papish, a friend and bird artist who wanted to learn banding, was also along. So I had to go up that trail.

Jefferson Park was, indeed, seven miles away, all uphill. It is one of the gems of the Cascade range. The mountain towers to ten thousand feet just to the south, with the snow line just above our camp that July. A couple of small lakes lie in the meadows, because the park area is essentially flat for perhaps a mile east to west. Rocky bluffs rise on the south end, and the eastern slope drops off into the Warm Springs Indian Reservation. We had permission from the Forest Service to band in the wilderness, but could not do so on reservation land.

The western approach to Jefferson is somewhat deceptive because most of it is within the forest and the final leg curls around a low shoulder before entering the open meadows of the parkland. We could certainly understand the reaction of early trekker Eaton, who had packed in by horse from Bend:

For two long days it had been our goal, and for two long days we had not seen it, not since we left the plain just out of Bend. Then it was many miles away. Now we were close upon it, and it burst into our vision alone, without a single rival, dominating the entire eastern sky, and seeming almost to rise out of a great bed of lupine and larkspur, of scarlet gilia and white mariposas.

The sun had sunk behind us, and the western ranges were filled with a purple light like some brilliant vapor flooding their canyons. Only on the higher snow-fields of the great mountain now did the direct rays linger; then they, too, lost their flash and sparkle, lost their amethyst flush, and stood chilly cold and white against the dusking sky.

Skyline Camps, Walter Prichard Eaton, 1922, p. 184-85

We had been hiking in through a single morning, not for two days, but I certainly felt as though I had been staggering along for days when we broke out into the open plateau. We set up camp where the climbers usually do and tried to site the pole-mounted nets where they seemed likely to be in whatever runs the owls might use.

We banded passerines during the daytime. There are few species in these high-elevation meadows, but juncos and Hermit Thrushes were fairly common. The most interesting daytime banding experience we had was when we set nets in an anomalous colony of Brewer's Sparrows. In theory there are no Brewer's Sparrows nesting in dwarf spruce at six thousand feet in Cascade alpine meadows, far from the nearest sagebrush, but we found at least six pairs. The habitat was unique: stunted spruce about four to five feet tall growing quite close together in a substrate of glacial gravel with limited soil and plenty of water from the mountain's runoff.

There is a form of Brewer's Sparrow known as Timberline Sparrow—considered by some a separate species—found in Canada. After our banding trip (which accidentally secured a specimen when one got tangled in a furled net overnight), we thought that this is what we might have found in the Cascades, but DNA tests showed that we had standard Brewer's Sparrows, an interesting piece of information in its own right. Later field work during the Oregon Breeding Bird Atlas project showed that the "desert" range of Brewer's Sparrow approaches the Cascade crest most closely in Jefferson County, right where we were.

Our night banding was based on the idea that Boreal Owls eat mice. We made two trips that summer up to Jefferson Park, and on the second one we brought along several pet-store mice in clear-plastic pastry containers. These were even more fun than net poles to maneuver up that long trail, though they did not weigh much. The plan was simple: set up the nets in likely flight lanes where Boreal Owls would be hunting. Place an obvious mouse in its escape-proof and marginally owl-proof container at the base of the net. Set up a flashlight to illuminate the bait. The owls will fly in after the mice and get caught in the net. We will remove and band the owls and science will triumph.

We caught no owls. I can't help thinking that the concept was sound, but that there were just no small owls in this location. We heard at least one Great Horned Owl, the presence of which would discourage small owls in an open-forest setting. I would not mind trying the idea again some time at a location where Boreal Owls are known to be—and which is closer than seven miles uphill.

1993: The Music of the Stars

One of my most prized books is my grandmother's signed copy of William O. Douglas's compendium of personal and wilderness stories, *Of Men and Mountains*, which Justice Douglas published in 1950, six years before I was born. This amiable collection of growing-up and mountain tales is a blurry mix of fact, fiction, and in-between (Douglas was a great one for in-between), but serves as a great introduction to the mountains of the Northwest, as does William Ashworth's *The Wallowas: Coming of Age in the Wilderness*, which I have read several times.

There are undoubtedly more Boreal Owls in the Wallowa Mountains of northeastern Oregon than in Jefferson Park. Far northeastern Oregon has a biological and geological character all its own. The mountains are the highest non-volcanic peaks in the state, really an outlier of the Rocky Mountain complex. From the north they rise almost vertically from the high grasslands and agricultural basins of Wallowa County, towering to nearly ten thousand feet in a broad crenellated massif twenty-five miles from east to west and almost that many north to south, merging into the ridgeline above Hells Canyon on the east and into the lower, older Blue Mountains to the west.

The Wallowa mountain region breathes of history. Chief Joseph was from this area—the town of Joseph bears his name. Lewis and Clark passed by not far to the north. Justice Willam O. Douglas had a cabin up the Lostine Valley, of which he wrote in *Of Men and Mountains*. This range has an allure common to mountains everywhere, and yet the special attraction described in Ashworth's classic *The Wallowas* is less common, indicative of a unique mystery, a magnetism that cannot be fully explained in words.

Much of the North American montane west consists of a mixture of agricultural valleys and adjacent mountain ranges. The Wallowa valley is in some ways typical of this region, biologically, socially, and economically more akin to Idaho or Montana than to the rest of Oregon. It is unfortunate that we from the urban areas of the west who visit these valleys tend to view the local resident human inhabitants as a form of indigenous fauna. Today Wallowa County is a curious mixture of traditional rural self-sufficiency and community on the one hand and an infusion of ex-urban yuppies on the other.

My college friend David Matthew was the Presbyterian minister in Lostine when I visited him in June 1993. Love took him away from Oregon; I doubt anything else could have. His ancestors were settlers in this valley.

I had Spruce Grouse and Pine Grosbeak on my mind because they were not on my list yet. I had last seen "Rev. Dave" in Fayetteville, Arkansas, a couple of years earlier. Now he had come back home to the place his family had settled decades earlier, and lived at the lower end of the Lostine Valley, just below the Wallowas. David is one of those people who appreciates the outdoors and birds with a small "b" but to whom Birding is a little over the top. Nonetheless he was willing to indulge an old friend and so I drove across the state one day (it takes eight hours to get from Eugene to Lostine) to see him.

The following morning he drove me to the trailhead for Brownie Basin, which Doug Lorain had recommended as a good place for Pine Grosbeak and possibly for Spruce Grouse. Doug is one of the Northwest's premier backpackers (author of *Backpacking Oregon* and *Backpacking Washington*) and knows his birds very well, so I had high hopes. The trail up to Brownie Basin begins very near Justice Douglas's cabin. Douglas wrote of his favorite retreat with precision and feeling:

An evening breeze swept off the mountain from the west. It carried the perfume of the snowbrush with it. That fragrance made this darkening canyon a place of enchantment, a land where only imagination can carry a man. Coming through Brownie Basin I had heard the wheezy notes of the White-crowned Sparrow. Now from some undisclosed thicket came the sweet song of Audubon's Hermit Thrush, the delicate singer who, as Gabrielson and Jewett once put it, produces "the music of the stars."
William O. Douglas, *Of Men and Mountains*, 1950

I had tried once before for Spruce Grouse up above the Lick Creek guard station on the east side of the Wallowas and had found Ruffed Grouse instead, though a superb view of an adult Goshawk made for a good consolation prize.

The riparian areas of Wallowa County in summer are a slice of the Rocky Mountains. Red-eyed Vireos are easy to find, singing even in the heat of midday; they are especially common in the Imnaha Valley. Dense streamside willow tangles harbor both Veery and Gray Catbird. The former is not a forest bird and the latter not a town bird in the west as they are in eastern North America. Perhaps the most attractive of these "eastern" birds is also the rarest, especially in recent years. The American Redstart can sometimes be found flitting delicately about in open mixed forests along streams.

Brownie Basin lies at about seven thousand feet. The floor of the Lostine canyon nearest to it is about five thousand feet. You see the problem. I had to go uphill again, this time on the Bowman Trail. According to Lorain's book, it is about 3.8 miles to the basin. However, the aspect of the trail was completely different from the brutal stagger up into Jefferson Park. The Jefferson Park trail goes more or less east all the way up. The trail into Brownie Basin is all switchbacks: it goes more or less straight up the slope of the canyon, back and forth, back and forth up through the pines and into the spruce-fir zone. It also has one great advantage over the Jefferson Park trail: the possibility of Pine Grosbeak and Spruce Grouse.

The other birds along the trail as I started up were all familiar. The constant flit of disturbed juncos. The occasional ethereal fluting of a ventriloquial Hermit Thrush, probably singing from the same dense thickets as when Justice Douglas heard them. Townsend's Warblers *zeedled* overhead from time to time. Partway up I rounded a bend and came face to face with a pack train coming downhill. The animals were accustomed to people so I was more shocked than they were as I stepped aside to let them pass.

As I went on up, the trail emerged onto an open hillside with an expansive view, and as I looked out across the opening I noticed two birds on a half-dead fir. Too big for crossbills. In fact an odd size for anything I had been seeing in the trees. They were a bit far off but through binoculars resolved themselves into an adult female and full-grown immature Pine Grosbeak—the only ones I saw until January of 2005.

Just before the trail finally gets serious about leaving the switchbacks and moving into the basin, Bowman Creek cuts down the side of the hill toward the side canyon over which the grosbeaks placidly sat. In the cluster of willows around the small pools of this stream a pair of Nashville Warblers had settled in. I was accustomed to seeing them in western Oregon, where they are common in drier habitats, especially in the interior southwest of the state, where they are one of the characteristic birds of hillside ceanothus patches. It seemed strange to find them in this quintessential wet habitat: a dense willow stand within an open spruce grove.

This was another example of the importance of structure over plant species in the vegetation that a bird uses. Willow sumps in northwestern Oregon don't contain Nashvilles, as a rule. Why not? Too wet owing to flatter terrain and heavier rainfall? Are the willows too large too often? These Bowman Creek willows had the same dense, somewhat stunted structure that a hillside of ceanothus would in southwestern Oregon. The presence of water did not seem a significant negative for this pair. I have found Nashvilles elsewhere in the Blue Mountains and near Upper Klamath Lake in similar settings.

As I wandered stiff-legged into the basin, no grouse did greet me. The basin is not flat as I had expected, but is a long hummocky meadow surrounded by a forest of spruce and fir. There are open fingers of grass and other fingers of forest along its western edge. It was under the fringe of one such stringer of trees that I pitched my tent.

Having hung my backpack where I thought bears were unlikely to get at it, I spent the afternoon wandering around the fringes of the basin sticking my head into likely thickets where grouse might be. This required some care, because too large a thicket approached too quietly might reveal a dozing black bear or even a cougar, which is best seen loping away at a reasonable distance, not tête-à-tête in the constrained maneuvering room of a dense stand of spruce, perhaps guarding young.

Being in a place like Brownie Basin overnight by myself was a new experience. As dusk settled on my grouseless day, the local pair of juncos had become accustomed to my tent, so as long as I sat in its entrance they would approach quite close, feeding their streaked sparrowy-looking young. A young junco can be one of the more confusing small birds in western forests, especially if the white outer tail feathers are not obvious. However, a quick mental check reveals what they are, mainly because the observer suddenly remembers: "I am in the middle of an evergreen forest at seven thousand feet in midsummer. There are no streaky sparrows here."

Although there were several other campers strung along the basin, the slightly uneven ground surface served to hide us from each other for the most part. As night laid its indigo veil across the trees, a great silence filled the basin. Above me as full dark fell, stars unknown in lower valleys shone through the high, clear air. How small I had felt even before looking up, alone in a black wilderness where I was, if relatively high on the potential food chain, not necessarily at its peak at that time and place.

Then to look up into the high glory, the ultimate music of the stars themselves. The unknowable extended for distances not truly conceivable by a human mind. What was I, in this place, after all?

I saw no Spruce Grouse going out the next day, either, and to this day have never seen one in Oregon. It does not matter.

Snow birds

I have been to Wallowa County as often in winter as in summer, and though the mountains look much the same—immense deep green giants covered with snow, visible at incredible distances across the region—the surrounding flatlands do not. Birders come to Wallowa County in winter because only here, a good eight hours from where most Oregon birders live, can the best variety of unique winter species be found.

Here Snow Buntings come in flocks rather than the dribbles of one or two that we sometimes find in western Oregon. Bohemian Waxwings are common in most winters, and Common Redpolls at least findable in most years. Gray Partridges scuttle from hedgerow to farmyard. American Tree Sparrows are often found in shrubby ditches in open country, while massive flocks of Gray-crowned Rosy-Finches move across the stubbled hillsides where there are no shrubs at all. One of Oregon's three records of Northern Hawk-Owl came from Union County just to the west.

Yet for all the finches and frugivores, it is the raptors that sometimes impress the most. These cultivated and native grassland expanses are the only place in Oregon where all five widespread falcons have been found in one day on a Christmas Bird Count. Gyrfalcon is all but annual, Rough-legged Hawks and Red-tails can be very common in open country, accipiters in the towns chasing robins, waxwings, and feeder-birds, Bald Eagles along the streams and Golden Eagles farther out, along the mountainsides and forest ridges.

One of the most impressive raptors of the Blue Mountains is the huge, puffy-looking Great Gray Owl. Many people see Great Grays in winter, but my only experience with this immense sack of feathers is in summer, most recently one that I saw near LaGrande, Oregon, with Trask Colby in August 2007. Little is more impressive than to come around a corner on a road through the pine forest and see a Great Gray staring at you from no great way across its meadow. And there is no doubt about whose meadow it is and who is the interloper.

Of all the raptors, the one that I enjoy most is the smallest: the towns, campgrounds, and forests of Wallowa County fill with Northern Pygmy-Owls in winter. Just about any time and place, a birder can get that funny feeling of being watched. A quick look around reveals a compact ball of potential perched on a wire, snag, or even building, staring this way and that with that look of disdainful irritation that only a pygmy-owl can manage.

For an observer from western Oregon, one of the odder experiences of birding in the Wallowa region is that, in a few places with plenty of moisture, a local population of Chestnut-backed Chickadees can be found. Perhaps the easiest place to find them is along the road that leads into Wallowa Lake State Park, though they occur west to the northwest edge of the Blue Mountains. They are different in more than location, being very reluctant to emerge and be seen.

1994: A Missourian Visits the West

I first met Jude Vickery during my second year in Missouri. He was eleven years old then, and had suddenly appeared on the birding scene by virtue of a combination of field skill and persistence. His ability to identify birds led him to conclude that the hummingbird coming to his feeder in early fall, 1989 was not a Ruby-throated—the only hummingbird that is supposed to occur in Missouri—but in fact a female Rufous. In fact the bird did prove to be a female *Selasphorus*, more likely Rufous than Allen's.

Jude wanted a more expert confirmation of the bird, so his persistence led him to call the Missouri Department of Conservation headquarters (about twenty miles away near Jefferson City) and talk his way through the bureaucracy until he reached Jim Wilson, the state ornithologist. Jim, knowing that this was not an ordinary eleven-year-old, went to Jude's house and saw the hummingbird himself. Then, not wanting to let a good young birder escape, Jim brought him to the Audubon Society of Missouri annual meeting at the Lake of the Ozarks. That is where I met him, as we were both trying to get looks at recalcitrant vireos.

Jude and I birded together occasionally in the two years I remained in Missouri, and when I left we discussed the possibility that someday he could come to the West and I could show him some new birds. This idea bubbled in my mind for a while after I moved back to Oregon in the fall of 1991, but I was planning my first trip to Arizona and was not sure how to do both.

After Jude's effort to sign up for a birding camp in Arizona fell through because of his parents' objection to the medical-treatment release form, I decided that it would be workable to combine my Arizona trip with Jude's western trip. He would fly to Oregon, we would bird here for several days, then drive to Arizona and spend a few days, with my friend Rich Hoyer, who was doing field work near Tucson, as our guide.

We could not make the trip before June 1994, and June is not the greatest birding month in Arizona, being very hot and lying between the two "spring" seasons of April and July, when moisture brings the desert to life. Nonetheless, neither of us had been there and we knew we would see a lot. Therefore when Jude's plane got to Portland, we were both ready for the first long-distance birding trip either of us had made, other than a brief trip I had taken to southern California in the early 1980s, when Kurt Radamaker, an old friend from Oregon, had shown me my first Black Skimmer, Vermilion Flycatcher, and other delights.

Our route began with elaborate loops through Oregon, during which Jude was able to find many new birds. Ocean birds such as lingering scoters, though perhaps the most exotic for a Midwesterner, did not excite him that much—perhaps birds can be *too* strange at times. One day when we stopped at a creek crossing near the town of Sisters, we saw the bird that got him most excited: a male Calliope Hummingbird perched on its usual willow twig. It had been his longtime fantasy to see this bird, and now it sat and preened at leisure.

This site has become so well known and is now visited so often by birders (including the 2003 American Birding Association convention tours) that it has become known as "Calliope Crossing," a better name by far than the dubious original Squaw Back Road or its successor, laughably formal for a gravel road in the forest, Pine Street. A harbinger of development, perhaps?

Our last stop in Oregon was my brother John's house in Medford near the California line. From there we had a long and largely birdless haul the next day: all the way to Bakersfield, California. The following day found us in habitat shockingly different from that of western Oregon: the Colorado River valley near Lake Havasu City. In addition to the change from snow in the Cascades to temperatures in the nineties and no humidity in the desert lowlands, the birds were different.

Not only were many of the species different, but even supposedly familiar species such as Canyon Wrens behaved differently compared to their Oregon congeners. As we walked into the shrubby flats of Bill Williams River wildlife area, the first bird I saw crawling about in a saltcedar was not a potential new bird for me about to emerge, but a Canyon Wren gleaning insects like a porcine vireo. It then flew over our heads to a nearby rock formation, where it was apparently feeding young. We saw several other Canyon Wrens behaving this way, which to this day I have never seen in Oregon, where Canyon Wrens have the good sense to remain in the rocks.

The flats of this wide wash did offer a few new birds, with Verdins passing deliberately through the shrubs and trees, a Brown-crested Flycatcher calling in the open (that is how new birds ought to behave), a Gila Woodpecker tapping on a sycamore, and White-winged Doves hurtling by, calling constantly in the background.

Verdins were a bit of a surprise for me, since I had expected them to act like Bushtits while in fact they were much more deliberate. Bushtits feed with desperate abandon, almost as though they are always being pursued and want one more bite to eat themselves before being eaten. What would bother to eat a Bushtit, animated fuzz with a tail stuck on as an afterthought? The energy expended in catching, disassembling, and swallowing one would surely exceed the caloric value of the intake, rather like a diet of celery for a human. A good master's thesis for someone.

Verdins disdain this adolescent frenzy, feeding actively, to be sure, but with a calmer sense of purpose and no sense that they need to be elsewhere *right now* that always seems to exude from Bushtits. There is a sense of rootedness with Verdins, a connection to place that a Bushtit never shows. Even in the breeding season, Bushtits are in such a hurry to build their outlandishly huge nests that breeding seems like a resented chore that has to be gotten over with quickly so the rhapsodic life of a wanderer can be continued. Not so the refined Verdin.

We spent one night in Lake Havasu City, where the ridiculous spectre of London Bridge crouched like a petrified reptile on the near horizon. We were not tempted to visit it, in fact nothing tempted me but a shower and a nap, so Jude saw a couple of birds that I didn't for a day or two by staggering around in the heat and flushing a Lesser Nighthawk, while a Ladder-backed Woodpecker graced the small local stand of trees.

The next day was mostly a travel day, getting us to Prescott, where we stayed the night with Doreen Dailey, president of Yavapai Community College, whom I had known when she was president at Clatsop Community College in Oregon a couple of years earlier. Doreen's home was in a nice thorn forest area north of town, and the following day she took us for the morning up to a nearby wilderness, where we got our first taste of Arizona pine country birds.

Oddly enough, our most noteworthy find that day was a breeding pair of Anna's Hummingbirds, nothing special on the West Coast but just then expanding into central Arizona. The trails and small pond yielded much Southwest exotica for both of us: Hepatic Tanagers in the forest, Phainopeplas in the larger openings, and Virginia's Warblers creeping uncooperatively about the dense shrub stands.

We reached Madera Canyon late the following day, and Rich was waiting for us in the parking area by our cabin. Broad-billed and Magnificent Hummingbirds swarmed the feeders and the calls of birds I had never heard before could be heard from the surrounding forest. I had a horrible headache, snarled at some old acquaintances from Missouri, and refused to go look at a Flame-colored Tanager because I wanted to lie down. After a period of recovery I went out with Rich and Jude and saw my first Sulphur-bellied Flycatcher, squealing away overhead. At dusk we heard and briefly saw a Whiskered Screech-Owl just behind the cabins, while the local Elf Owl emerged from its hole in a utility pole in front.

That night after dark we walked out toward Florida Wash, a dry wash below the road that goes up to the Madera Canyon cabins. As far as I could tell, this stroll was intended to be A Blind Person's

Guide to the Cacti, or perhaps a seminar on how to tell venomous reptiles apart by the sound of their slithering. I'm sure I heard at least a dozen scorpions right along the "path," which as far as I could tell was marked only because it was the direction that Rich was walking between the ocotillos and barrel cacti.

That path eventually led to the edge of the wash, where we heard the night chorus of the Sonoran desert: a pulsating carpet of Common Poorwills, present by the dozens as far as the ear could hear, with counterpoint by a nearby pair of Western Screech-Owls. But close in front of us was the sound we had hoped for: the "chuck-chuck-chuckatakreeer" of a Buff-collared Nightjar. It is unlikely that I will ever *see* a Buff-collared Nightjar, but if I do, I doubt that it will give me quite the sense of sitting in on an entirely different world that I felt upon first hearing that strange accelerating churr over the other night birds in the dark of Florida Wash.

In the morning—the *early* morning—we started up the loop trail that goes up to the saddle south of the resort. At first, there was little bird activity along the trail, then suddenly a face peered from a trailside tree: a Bridled Titmouse was checking to see if we were interesting. The result seemed to be neutral, as it soon went about its business, allowing us good looks as we went up, up, and more up. Within a mile, the quiet was broken by warbler call notes, and Rich started his imitation Ferruginous Pygmy-Owl calls. Up from the dim canyon below boiled an astonishing array of birds. Sudden first looks: the unlikely head of a Red-faced Warbler—and there were half a dozen of them, astonishing at first look and still astonishing every time I have seen them since. Painted Redstarts glowed whenever they appeared. Grace's Warblers popping out of every pine, more titmice. A glorious introduction to the pine country of southern Arizona.

Farther up the trail a sudden movement overhead caught our eye. A pair of Arizona Woodpeckers had been sitting quietly; now they moved around an oak, allowing us the only views I would have until the spring of 2003. As we watched the woodpeckers, we heard The Sound. It was the sound we had fantasized about for years, unlike anything else in North America. It echoed up from the depth of the canyon and was suddenly answered from ahead of us, some way off. Trogons!

How does one actually *see* a trogon? Well, that year we did not have to look for them by following their calls, which was a good thing because they were at the bottom of a canyon and we were halfway up the side of it, with nothing but rocks, thorny shrubs, venomous spiders, and serpents in between. As we rounded the next turn in the trail, a male trogon suddenly flew up from below, perched twenty feet to our right gazing at us, then launched itself in a loose, headlong flight across the trail and off into the forest.

We took a moment to recover from having golden eggs strewn upon us. A little giddy, we walked on up the trail, emerging into a fairly open area from which we could see the far ridgetop. A clear, whistled song drifted down from somewhere up there.

"Greater Pewee." Rich was very matter-of-fact about it, but of course he had seen plenty of them. We could see it after a fashion, on the tip of a snag across the canyon and above us. This view was the only one I would have for several years, but combined with the quite audible song it made for a good experience.

It was not long after that, as we approached the summit ridge where several trails converged, that a darting shape in the shadows below alerted us to the presence of Yellow-eyed Juncos. These birds have such a different facial appearance that they don't seem close kin to the Dark-eyed Juncos that we see all the time in the Northwest. The brilliant yellow eye and a hint of eyebrow impart a strangely malevolent glare to them. The placid feeder-birds or montane tent-companions of home could never look like this. Yet in behavior they are quite junco-like, though shyer than other juncos.

Coming down the back side of the canyon we chanced upon a Painted Redstart nest when I walked too close to the embankment beside the trail. The nest was about two feet above the trail, concealed under overhanging leaves, and seemed to be in a cluster of roots and rocks. Seen up close, a Painted Redstart has a certain velvet loveliness that few warblers can match.

Patagonia

On that trip we had one of the fortuitous experiences that makes birding a source of endless pleasure. As we arrived at the famous Patagonia wayside after seeing a horde of hummingbirds at the Paton's feeder, other birders were wandering about in the trees in a state of anticipation too long maintained. Their eyes were a little glassy, smiles just that slight bit forced, movements occasionally jerky as though they would duck right through another person.

The reason became apparent: they had *not yet seen* the female Yellow Grosbeak that had been in the area in previous days. Only Guy McCaskie seemed his usual self, carrying the air of a skeptical badger that has been his hallmark for decades, and a good cover for his genuine enthusiasm for finding a new bird—he hadn't dropped into these trees from San Diego by accident.

As all experienced birders know, the most important word in birding is the word "yet." We had no fantasies about Yellow Grosbeaks because they are so rare a Mexican vagrant that we had never thought of seeing one. That allowed us to quickly announce, "There it is," as the bird flew behind the assembled birders, all of whom spun about and devoured it with their eyes as it sat briefly in the open, showing off its immense bill, before going deeper into the undergrowth.

A wave of contentment sifted through the crowd, and they were happy to show us the nests of Violet-crowned Hummingbird and Rose-throated Becard that we had come to see. A Thick-billed Kingbird came to a treetop across the creek to add to the occasion. And I think Guy smiled, I really think I saw it.

Bird 500

We stopped at several more locations and saw a lot of interesting birds, but it was at the Nogales sewage ponds that I saw my five-hundredth species of North American bird. Sewage ponds can be great birding spots because they are often the only sizable bodies of water in a given area—especially the desert—and they are somewhat protected from human disturbance. There is even a birders' site guide to the sewage ponds of my home state, Oregon.

As we drove in we came across the odd spectacle of a Northern Beardless-Tyrannulet and a Varied Bunting sitting on the metal fence around the ponds. We had seen both of these birds earlier, though not better. Neither sits on fences in the open very often. It was a good omen. At first there was not much else, then Bird 500 showed itself, or rather themselves: a small flock of Black-bellied Whistling-Ducks idled on the mud.

Shortly after that watershed event we heard a buzzer go off and a truck with plant workers came past us. We inquired as to whether there was a problem, and one of them answered with considerable gravity:

"We have a situation."

Well, we could hardly argue with that, and we have used that phrase a number of times since when other "situations" came about.

Now there's an orthodontist

Our return trip featured a brutal climb out of Needles, California, with an outside temperature around 108 degrees. We eventually had to turn off the air conditioner in order to keep the engine temperature within reasonable bounds. The transition from desert fauna to urban fauna can best be illustrated by the last glimpse of a roadrunner in the morning and the first sight of singer Madonna's home in the evening, seen from the terrace of the home where we were staying with my college friend Albert and his then-partner Sherwin.

Albert and Sherwin lived high on the Hollywood hillside, with Anna's Hummingbirds zipping over the hedges and a male Phainopepla making figure-eight loops over the hillside below. Madonna's towers showed above the trees about three blocks away, and Jude emerged from the swimming pool long enough to look in that direction with the mixture of admiration and doubt that a religious sixteen-year-old might be expected to show:

> *He took home and to church*
> *that craggy pagan vision,*
> *looming in vermilion twilight,*
> *of the castle*
> *of the goddess.*

Visiting Sherwin and Albert was also culturally broadening in another way for Jude. Although he knew I was gay, visiting a gay couple was a little different, especially because of the anecdote that Albert shared with us as we sat around the pool. It seemed that their neighbor beyond the hedge had known the previous owners, also gay, and did not much like them. The neighbor was apparently clueless about the current inhabitants, for he'd been overheard saying that "the place used to be owned by a couple of homosexuals, but now an orthodontist lives there."

We did not see many new birds or identifiable orthodontists on the rest of the way home, though a lengthy encounter with Yellow-billed Magpies at an obscure highway rest area finally persuaded Jude that they existed, and he acquired an unseemly smugness at the notion of showing his close-up photos of them to a fellow Missouri birder who had never been able to find them during his California visits.

1995: Valleys in the Sun

My journal has a short but bird-full entry for Independence Day, 1995, which was a birding day with a purpose:

July 4, 1995. Breeding Bird Atlas trip to South Baker County and North Grant County with Bryan Ledford. We found several Willow Flycatchers along the creek south of Baker City. Found breeding White-throated Swifts and a singing "Cordilleran" Flycatcher in the central Burnt River Canyon. This area also has lots of Lewis' Woodpeckers. Camped at Eldorado south of Unity, lots of Hammond's Flycatchers in camp area. Atlas run behind Ironside Mountain produced lots of woodpeckers. Vaux's Swifts seem absent here—why? Stayed the night in John Day, did atlas run in northwest Grant County next day. Great birding at park and pond complex in Monument.

Oregon has so many interesting corners that I will never see all of them, but the Burnt River Canyon that runs from southeast of Baker City up toward Unity stands out. It is not that long—some twenty-five miles from near Durkee up to the junction with Highway 245. The road is mostly good-quality gravel and there is little traffic. It begins in farm and ranch land. We found no Bobolinks here, but the habitat could support them in wet years. The lower part of the road traverses a mix of big sagebrush, semi-cleared grasslands and drier ranchlands.

It then moves quickly up into hills that support the kind of eclectic mix of micro-habitats that can be found in parts of eastern Oregon. Patches of mountain mahogany and juniper on the drier slopes intermingle with swaths of ponderosa pine and even some Douglas-fir at the western (higher) end of the canyon, with willows and cottonwoods along the narrow river. Snowberry and chokecherry add to the mix in narrow draws, and sagebrush fingers extend wherever they can.

This is Lazuli Bunting country, and also supports plenty of Yellow-breasted Chats where the riparian growth is sufficiently dense. Unknown to most Oregonians, this valley and nearby areas have one of the continent's greatest densities of breeding Lewis's Woodpecker. They might as well be dubbed "Sluggish Flycatcher" as be called woodpeckers. They lurch and sideslip from tree to tree all along the canyon and in the more open areas up near Unity. Anywhere an old apple tree left over from a homestead can be found, it is likely to contain a couple of Lewis's Woodpeckers hopping and creeping from branch to branch.

At one location halfway up the canyon, the road rises somewhat above the river and it is possible to look south across the river to a cliff face that is on eye level. This is where we had the unusual experience of watching a single pair of White-throated Swifts going in and out of their presumed nest crack, also at eye level. I was so accustomed to watching these swifts far, far above, moving at high speed or simply disappearing behind pillars, that it was fascinating to watch them flutter to a landing, if such a phrase can be applied to a bird with essentially no feet.

They flew right up to the cliff face and folded their wings on impact, as it were, with the front of the bird usually inside the crack. We could not see quite how they propelled themselves into the crack, but it was done in a quick scuttle, perhaps with toes and wing edges. A moment later, out one would come, first a vision of a pale face and then a burst of flight. The cliff was small and only held one pair.

Just below the swift crack and slightly downstream, a male Cordilleran Flycatcher, if there is such a species after Western Flycatcher was split, sang repeatedly. This is the only location in Oregon where I have ever heard a bird that gave only the "proper" Cordilleran songs. As a birder I can therefore list it, and its existence is thereby confirmed. The habitat was a combination of riparian willows and cottonwoods in a fairly open setting; there were no evergreens present.

Ray's ride

These sun-washed valleys of far eastern Oregon have been in my family, in a manner of speaking, for nearly a hundred years. My maternal grandparents, Ray and Berta Barker, homesteaded for a time just below Mt. Fanny on the outskirts of Cove, in Union County. My grandfather, who was born in 1893 in Mentor, Minnesota, lived a little more than one hundred years and I recall many conversations with him that seemed to span the history of the United States. In fact, his life spanned close to half of it, and I recall the shimmer of awe that came over me the first time I realized that he could have met someone who had known Thomas Jefferson personally. We once talked of his clear memories of the Roosevelt election for a few minutes before I realized that he was referring to Theodore, not Franklin, Roosevelt.

Ray Barker grew up in a time before cars, and during one of the brief periods in his life that he had spare time (as a farmer and orchardist, he did not have guaranteed vacation days), he decided to visit the Catlow Valley in south-central Oregon. I do not know what prompted this decision. When we talked of it he simply mentioned that he had gone there. This was probably just after his service in World War I, which concluded happily when his ship turned around in mid-Atlantic on Armistice Day. Ray married Berta Kirk in November 1916, and his trip was after their marriage, probably between 1918 (after the war) and 1920.

In the period between 1913 and 1921, the road network in eastern Oregon expanded considerably. However, a man on horseback is not limited to travel by roads, paved or unpaved, and may well want to avoid such surfaces. From Cove to the Catlow Valley is about two hundred miles, whether you go via the Malheur River Valley or via John Day.

I like to fantasize that Ray Barker took the Malheur River route (I never thought to ask him), because by so doing he would have retraced a chunk of the Oregon Trail while heading south over the summit via Telocaset and North Powder (the main route went that way early in the century, not through Ladd Canyon as it does now).

My fantasy continues with the solitary horseman following the main track in the Powder River valley, then heading over the Burnt River Mountains ridge to the southwest following the draw of Durbin Creek, as I did many years later. The creek would provide water for half of the distance. Then over the low summit, dropping down into Willow Creek valley near Brogan, stopping for the night at a welcoming ranch. The first welcoming ranch seen by someone coming down the canyon and emerging at Brogan was owned at that time by my friend Mary Anne Sohlstrom's grandparents, so I like to imagine

White-crowned and whte-throated sparrows. Ramiel Papish

my grandfather spending the night there. An early ornithologist described this region:

This lower portion of the valley has been in ranches for many years, and a considerable part of it is devoted to alfalfa raising. About the ranch houses are considerable orchards and shrubbery and tall Lombardy poplars, forming a favorite resort for a number of species, which were here found in great abundance. Furthermore, large numbers of Fringillidae were noted in the extensive patches of sunflowers, the seeds of which, when in season, probably formed their principal food. In Willow Creek Canyon birds were found in only moderate numbers, but in the little canyon of Pole Creek both species and individuals were abundant.

The avian life of the dry, sage-brush-covered hills appeared to be in general rather plentiful.

Morton E. Peck, *Summer Birds of the Willow Creek Valley*, 1910

The Willow Creek valley looks today much as Morton Peck describes it, which means that my grandfather, if he took that logical route, would, upon leaving Brogan, have passed down a valley of many small ranches extending from the creek into sage flats and hillsides. Brogan was a more important site in comparative economic terms then than it is now, for the Oregon Short Line railroad spur went as far as Brogan and stopped.

Where would a solitary horseman of ninety years ago go next, if he wanted to visit the Catlow Valley? The same way we would travel today, by turning west along the Malheur River valley. This, in the years immediately after World War I, was not the principal road west from Vale as it is today. The main route was what we know today as the Bully Creek road leading to Westfall, which then continued westward, then south to the Beulah townsite (just south of where Beulah Reservoir is today) and on to Drewsey and Burns. This route is still passable today with a high-clearance vehicle under dry conditions.

The southern route was almost all desert, looping past the old Creston townsite and eventually reaching Riverside before crossing the hills into Crane and the Harney basin. Only the western portion of this route is still easily driven. I think Ray would have followed the central, more rustic Malheur River route through Harper and

Juntura instead. It would follow a larger stream for fishing and join the southern route at Riverside. East of Juntura, this is in part the same route that U.S. 20 follows today.

This is one of the most beautiful parts of Oregon, seen best by those who live there, or by a slow-moving horseman. The river, edged by willows and cottonwoods, provides fishing as well as an opportunity to watch herons, orioles, waxwings, and perhaps Sharp-tailed Grouse (until the 1950s) or Sage Grouse (local today) and Mountain Quail (all but absent today). Chukars, one of the common birds of the region today (used as the namesake of athletic teams at Treasure Valley Community College), were not introduced until 1930. Ray would not have seen any.

As he traveled west of Vale, he might have visited at the ranch now owned by Bob Kindschy and his family. Bob was my co-author of *Birds of Malheur County* and his family has been in the county for decades. The ranch is good bottomland with stands of cottonwood, willow, and juniper.

Ray Barker may have stayed at other ranches along the way, or may have camped along the river, fished for his dinner, and slept under the cottonwoods. The Western Screech-Owls I have heard along the river may be descended from those that he heard. I imagine that he heard Poorwills calling from the sage-covered bluffs after dark, and watched as nighthawks "peented" over the river, hawking for moths.

Along the canyons further west, as the river winds out of the agricultural lowlands, he might have seen White-throated Swifts—or perhaps not, as biologist Edward Preble did not see them in 1915 north of Watson (now submerged) on the Owyhee River south of where present-day Leslie Gulch meets the reservoir. They were not reported in the canyons of central Oregon until the 1950s. But he would have noticed the Violet-green, Cliff, and Barn Swallows that use natural habitats all along the route, and perhaps an occasional Rock Wren bobbing along the road.

The pocket valley of Juntura was settled then, and would have made a natural stopping place as well, with a mix of farmsteads, pastureland, and open sage country. Western Kingbirds would have greeted him as he rode into the valley's northeastern corner. Magpies may have watched him come with an eye to stealing some lunch.

Malheur County revisited

My own ride into the rough country of northern Malheur County on June 14-15, 1995, started out just fine but when I tried to get past Beulah Reservoir I could have used a horse. I went to eastern Oregon to get more information for the book on Malheur County and to do atlasing as part of the Oregon Breeding Bird Atlas project.

I stayed the first night at the Malheur Field Station. Nothing special was at headquarters in the evening. The morning of the 15th there was a female Northern Parula by the restroom. It was silent; I saw it go by into the adjacent hawthorn, or I never would have known it was there.

I drove north via Princeton to Buchanan, seeing lots of Horned Larks and Red-tails and a nice view of Swainson's Hawk north of Crane. Going east on Highway 20 to the impoundment along the highway near Stinkwater Creek, I was off the historic routes, which had generally followed water, not gone straight up and down dry hills. This year, however, there was lots of water in the valleys along the highway. Coots and Mallards had young. Wilson's Phalaropes, Cinnamon Teal, Blue-winged Teal, and Black-necked Stilt were easy to find.

I was back on the old northern route at Chukar Park north of Juntura for lunch. This is a significant and underappreciated gem among the many jewels in the crown of eastern Oregon parks and campgrounds. It was full of mating waxwings and goldfinches. Yellow-breasted Chats hollered from the densest growth, and a pair of Downy Woodpeckers was prospecting, perhaps for a second brood.

The upper end of Beulah Reservoir where Warm Springs Creek comes in had an incredible bird concentration. Yellow-headed Blackbirds were apparently breeding in inundated willows, showing again the importance of structure over plant type. An amazing eleven species of duck seemed to be breeding there—Green-winged, Cinnamon, and Blue-winged Teal, Lesser Scaup (ten pair), Mallard, American Wigeon (two pair), Gadwall, Ruddy Duck, Ring-necked Duck, Northern Pintail, Northern Shoveler—plus many Western Grebe (twelve pair), some displaying. Other notables at Beulah that day were Osprey, Wilson's Phalarope, Forster's Tern, Great Egret, and Wilson's Snipe.

That is when I entered horse country but kept driving: I went west along the north side of the reservoir and up the bad road along the Malheur River. This is good riparian habitat containing Spotted Towhees, Western Kingbirds, and more chats.

Unfortunately it is no place for a low-slung Plymouth or any other passenger car: I destroyed a tire. Oh, for a horse, could I have but ridden it. I tried when I was sixteen, at the instigation of my friend Bob Hanks, lost recently at too young an age, but the horse ignored what I thought I told it to do (undoubtedly a tribute to the horse's good judgment) and cantered downhill at what seemed a frightening speed to get back to the grass it wanted to be in.

No quiet horseman out of my mythic past appeared on the desert road to show me the trail and lend me a mount. I managed to get back down the hill to Juntura and fled east to Ontario.

On June 16, I left Ontario early and drove up the highway toward Ironside, crossing Ray Barker's route at Willow Creek near Brogan, and started up Forest Road 16 about 6:30. The habitat is excellent pine with fir intermixed; aspen and willow strings are narrow and patchy. I went up King Creek Road and soon ran into recently burned areas. A Northern Pygmy-Owl was hooting and hunting from dense fir along the road. On the south side of the mountain, the aspen grove 1.6 miles south of the saddle on Bridge Creek Road (bottom of the second switchback) was excellent: eighteen species of birds were using that one stand and adjacent pines.

A pair of Williamson's Sapsuckers, so unalike as to have been originally treated as two species, were either prospecting for a nest hole or recovering from a first brood, or both. A pair of White-breasted Nuthatches, sounding so different from the ones in western Oregon, worked their way up, in, around, down, and across any available tree. A Warbling Vireo sang constantly and a Western Wood-Pewee called its depressed meow just down the hill.

At the bottom of the hill was the so-called junction leading west, eventually to the alleged road north of Beulah, or east down Willow Creek to Ironside and the highway. Discretion led me to the highway. The intersection of Bridge Creek Road and South Willow Creek is poorly marked, but the directions are easy to figure out.

Willow Creek is edged in dense riparian willows, with a few other trees and shrubs scattered in. It is towhee country. In certain parts of eastern Oregon, Green-tailed and Spotted Towhees intermix along desert riparian zones with good cover, and Willow Creek sports the odd sight of Green-tailed Towhees lurking in willows above the creek while Spotted Towhees creep about in stands of big sagebrush and mountain mahogany, the reverse of what bird books would lead us to expect.

These towhees are not the warm, confiding trillers of western Oregon garden and feeder. They are the less common interior subspecies *curtatus*, a "wild" towhee in every way, and often difficult to see, taking after their congener Green-tails. They also sound different, with more notes than the flat rattle of Willamette Valley birds.

The rest of that trip was uneventful, long hauls of highway with not much opportunity to get off into the country.

1999: Listing for a Purpose

There are all sorts of birding events, some mainly fun, some scientifically useful, and a few birding for a purpose. One of the most fun is a Big Day, and it can be combined with doing good, as in the wild experiences on the University of Oregon Museum of Natural History Birdathon. This was a fundraiser for the museum.

Saturday, May 15, 1999

3:00 a.m. I have not done a Big Day in twenty years and my body thought it would never have to do another one: this is a heck of a time to be awake on a perfectly good day for sleeping in. But this is when I get to Jeff Marx's driveway and find him standing in the dark in his birding gear like the Mummy of the South Hills, ready to engage in his first west coast Big Day. He's done many in the northeastern U.S., so he can't say he doesn't know what he's getting into. His fiancée may already be awake too, but then, she's still in New York.

We're trying to break the Lane County Big Day Record (153, set in 1983) and we would not mind breaking the western Oregon record of 160, though it involved more than one county. And the meter is ticking: for each species we find, the University of Oregon Museum of Natural History will receive about sixteen dollars in pledges. And we get to spend an entire day avoiding our chores.

3:30 Dave Irons is waiting at Shari's Restaurant on River Road, pumping coffee into his arteries and wondering whether this is all a joke and we won't pick him up at all. He was a member of Oregon's all-time record Big Day team that found 212 species on a coast-to-Malheur run in the early 1980s—we wouldn't set him up, would we? Nah. If we don't get to sleep in, neither does he. As we open the car door to let him in, he grins and points upward: Swainson's Thrushes are migrating—our first bird of the day is checked off: the same species with which I started twenty-three years earlier.

4:30 We try known and unknown sites for Barn Owl north of the Eugene airport and come up empty. After an abortive prowl around Alvadore on our way west, we park at the summit of Cougar Pass between Noti and Walton in the middle of the Coast Range. Owling involves listening to various night noises (distant dogs, creeks babbling over rocks, Sasquatch belching) and convincing yourself that these muffled hooting or hissing noises are actually several species of owls to be added to the day's tally. We also imitate owls in order to lure them into responding; the conventional wisdom suggests that their responses consist of the avian equivalent of laughter at our efforts. Eventually we get one distant Northern Pygmy-Owl to respond, but by now robins are singing and we know dawn is not far off.

5:45 We are on the Clay Creek access road in the central Coast Range. The forest and the open area are starting to emit bird sounds as Chestnut-backed Chickadees, Spotted Towhees, and MacGillivray's Warblers come to life in the predawn dimness. This is our first shot at some woodland birds before we spend most of the morning on the outer coast. We hope to get some unpredictable species: grouse or Mountain Quail. We don't. However, a Northern Pygmy-Owl comes in and looks at us and then, with a squeal of discord, two pygmy-owls pounce on each other in the road right by us. Now that's territorial.

6:30 We can see well enough now that as we arrive at the parking area by the confluence of the North Fork of the Siuslaw River, we see birds over the mudflats and estuary. Western Gulls cruise along and crows pour off the hillsides and onto the mudflats, where some early clammers have taken the space we hoped would be burdened with shorebirds. Some careful scoping yields a good bounty though: both species of yellowlegs, some Short-billed Dowitchers, and a Spotted Sandpiper are lining the shores of a far island. A Band-tailed Pigeon tears along over the hillside. As we leave we remark on the absence of kingfishers along the river all the way from Mapleton.

7:00 As daylight gets serious we are the first people to waddle out the dike into the deflation plain behind the dunes of the Siuslaw estuary, pursuing American Bittern and other waterbirds. At the end of the dike we'll see waterfowl and shorebirds if we are lucky. The Bittern, Virginia Rail, and Sora cooperate magnificently, and our only Bufflehead (rather late) are sailing along in the flooded basin. Savannah Sparrows zip away into the grass.

8:00 The south jetty of the Siuslaw is our first crack at seabirds and "rockpipers," whose preferred habitat is coastal rocks and jetties. But it is a late migrant land bird that first gets our attention: As we walk toward the jetty, a dry call drifts to our ears. Dave stops: "Isn't that a longspur?" I hear it, too, and a quick search reveals at least two Lapland Longspurs in the grass. One hops up onto a log, showing its spring colors partly molted in. This is a "bonus bird" that will help make up for the poor owl showing. We dash out the jetty and run up a serious list of seabirds, calling out to each other: "Marbled Murrelets—Red-throated Loon—Wandering Tattler," and also find another semi-bonus: a Herring Gull that might easily have been in Canada by now. However, we miss both Black Turnstone and Surfbird, which we can only get here or at other rocky spots. A few ought to still be here this late in May. A memorable sight: Ten Ospreys kettling over the Siuslaw jetties, where one would have been noteworthy when I started birding in the late 1960s. What a comeback.

9:30 The north fork of the Siuslaw is a delightfully swampy place. Here we come to search for quackers: various freshwater dabbling ducks such as teal and wigeon that have mostly gone north by now. Mostly. It's the tag ends of "mostly" that we're after in these mucky pastures. We manage to extract some Northern Shovelers and, at the boat ramp, Golden-crowned Kinglets.

9:40 A quick stop to peer into Sutton Lake, where we find nothing at all. This is a good spot in winter, but on a nice morning in May there are boaters, not floaters.

9:45 We are running behind so skip the Baker Beach road swamp. A tactical decision that probably does no harm. We did not have time to walk out for Snowy Plovers anyway, and we already have rails.

10:00 We are at one of our crucial stops: Devil's Elbow State Park. Here we should find Tufted Puffins barely visible on the offshore rock, as well as hypothetical dippers up Cape Creek. We find the puffins, not the dippers. We also see a large brown bird burst from low foliage and crash into the shrubbery up Cape Creek—a grouse?! No, an extremely out-of-place Red-tailed Hawk. Granted, our first of the day, but what was it doing lurching through the bushes a foot off the ground like a demented goshawk? Chasing aplodontia? Back to the rocks: can we find a Black Oystercatcher, or have we lost it for the day? None.

10:45 Sea Lion Caves is right next door as we peer down the cliff into the colonies of Brandt's Cormorants and hundreds of pairs of Pigeon Guillemots. On the water below is the real prize of this unassuming overlook: Rhinos ! Well, not the big ones. These are less than a foot long: Rhinoceros Auklets, which breed inside the caves and in very few other places in Oregon. We hope for Black Swift, a semi-predictable migrant that comes through in small numbers and often moves right along coastal cliffs. None, but Dave spots (at a distance of about eight miles) a circling Sharp-shinned Hawk over the coastal bluffs and we all peer through the scope at it. It will prove our only one of the day. Below—straight down, in fact—on the rocks are a few Black Oystercatchers.

11:30 At the North Jetty of the Siuslaw, the mudflats are mostly underwater now and we make one more pass for shorebirds missed in the morning. Where are those pesky turnstones? Elsewhere, today. We never find them, though a semi-bonus appears in the form of a single Ruddy Turnstone that appears at the tip of the south jetty. We scope it in the hope that it brought cousins. None. A Ring-billed Gull is a good consolation prize, too: we will finish the day with six gull species, by no means assured in mid-May.

12:15 It's time to start inland, where an entirely different set of birds awaits. Our tally as we leave the coast is 110. We've missed some but picked up others, so we are confident of making the high 130s, but doubtful about the county record: 153.

1:15 After zooming through the Coast Range with a brief unsuccessful side jaunt (still no dipper) and a change of drivers (I have been behind the wheel since 3:00 a.m.), we slide into the parking area on Highway 126 by Fern Ridge Reservoir. Are the Yellow-headed Blackbirds willing to appear? Instantly. As are coots.

1:30 Perkins Peninsula Park, usually a gold mine in spring migration, does not disappoint. Here we find our first Chipping Sparrows and a Clark's Grebe, which breeds only here in all of western Oregon. The real bonus comes as we scope the far reedbeds northeast of Perkins: Black Terns, an uncommon local breeder, flap lazily by, two Bald Eagles soar overhead, and finally Dave latches onto fifteen Redhead, all paired up on the water as if to breed. Except that they don't breed in western Oregon. Until perhaps now. A great and unexpected find.

3:45 South of Fern Ridge the countryside is fairly open in spots, and we look along Nielson and Cantrell roads for Western Kingbird. We find one almost instantly, along with our first American Kestrel of the day. Close to the Coyote Creek area we hope for Red-shouldered Hawks but find none. However, a Vesper Sparrow sings just up the hill and a Bullock's Oriole goes "chack!" from the trees.

4:15 We make a quick check of the oak groves and nearby grassy areas at the western end of Royal Avenue, gathering up Acorn Woodpecker and Western Meadowlark.

4:30 Stewart Pond is a complex of gooey areas and open water in west Eugene. It could be our make-or-break stop, as far as getting to the record is concerned. It is a solid stop: our first Green Heron, American Wigeon, Green-winged Teal, House Wren, and Ring-necked Pheasant.

5:00 Skinner's Butte: an unlikely piece of good habitat smack in the center of Eugene, but here we need to find Anna's Hummingbird and Lesser Goldfinch. Also, the butte is a migrant magnet sticking up from downtown, and anything could be there. We know that this hill has been sucking in migrants for days; we also know that to get close to 150 we need to find *all* of them: there is no room for error. Half an hour later we have had a remarkable run of luck generated in large part by the recent experience of Dave and Jeff birding the butte. We add to the list Hermit Thrush, Hutton's Vireo, Cassin's Vireo, Red-breasted Nuthatch, Hammond's Flycatcher, Pacific-slope Flycatcher, Anna's hummer, Lesser Goldfinch, and the most remarkable find of all, a male Calliope Hummingbird, a rare west-side migrant that we did not expect at all.

Jeff, who has never seen one in his life, being a recent transplant from New York, spots it hovering almost overhead and we identify it with amazement. It is the first Calliope Dave has ever seen in western Oregon. Nine new birds at one whack moves us into the 140s and we realize that there is just a chance that we can not only reach 150 but break the record, 153. We have been birding for fourteen hours.

5:45 Ah, the Lane Community College sewage ponds, none so fair. There have been Ruddy Ducks here, and these ponds are well known as drop-in sites for all manner of migrant waterbirds. We hope to pick up a stray or two. As we zip down the off-ramp, a hawk drifts over the nearby woods and flaps unenthusiastically to the west. Another sharp-shin. NO! It's a Cooper's Hawk! We all get good views. The Ruddy Ducks are there.

LCC is the end of the formal route that I planned to take advantage of the county's habitats, allowing some hunting time for missing birds. We are short on birds of brushy hillsides, but otherwise we've had a great day. We are at 147 species, with better than two hours of light left. But our missing birds are separated all over the county (except for the ubiquitous yet absent—can such a phrase be used?—Belted Kingfisher). There is no one place to go for more than perhaps two of them. We settle on a huge circle that will allow us to be back at Royal Avenue at dusk in the hope of Great Horned Owl and even conceivably Barn or Short-eared Owl.

6:00 We dash down the freeway to Creswell, then dash back north to be able to pull over next to a lovely slime pit along the northbound lanes of the highway near Short Mountain Landfill. Dave had seen shorebirds there in previous days and we hope to pick up Dunlin or perhaps Black-bellied Plover. As we drive up, at least two sizes of birds are present, including two we already have, Killdeer and Least Sandpiper, plus a few Green-winged Teal, which we also have. But the two Wilson's Phalaropes are a real bonus—they are not common migrants in western Oregon. 148. I try to convert a female teal to a Long-billed Dowitcher (it was already a long day) but it does not remain discreetly hidden in the grass and I do not succumb to the Dark Side of the Force.

6:30 The east side roads and lower trail at Mt. Pisgah could theoretically produce Western Bluebird, Nashville Warbler, Lazuli Bunting, and a few other things we are missing. As we drive down the twisting road, Dave spots a small wire-sitter that proves to be a Western Wood-Pewee, which we had hoped for but which had been held up a little in migration. 149. A quick prowl along the roads reveals no bluebirds, but as we walk out the trail we start seeing lots of sparrows and hearing songs.

I name a beautiful sprightly uplifting distant song to be that of a glorious Lazuli Bunting (150), but as we draw closer it is clearly the insipid uncoordinated directionless babble of a scuzzy already-listed American Goldfinch. However, I redeem myself by detecting, as we walk out to the car, a clear whistled song from across the road. I pronounce the name slowly as the others perk up: Ca-li-for-nia-Quail. A real 150.

7:15 We are now clearly within range of the record but it is very late in the day. We decide to continue with our circle and make a quick pass out Van Duyn Road and a side road in the hope of bunting, Western Bluebird, and maybe Wild Turkey. We find more American Goldfinches, a perfectly gorgeous bird that I now find deeply unattractive, and some Lesser Goldfinches, but nothing new.

7:45 The desperate dash westward from Coburg to Fern Ridge Dam (a last chance for the absurdly wayward kingfisher) involves a lot of looking out windows for Cedar Waxwing (another missed bird) and a disconsolate glower at the McKenzie and Willamette rivers where kingfishers could zoom by but do not. We are alert as we drive up to Kirk Pond at the dam. What is that on the wire? A fishing bobber. What is in the pond—a late migrant scaup? A nice grebe? An unexpected Canvasback? Nothing at all. As we drive toward the dam we know that we have to have at least one good break here in the warm evening to tie, let alone break, the record. I am driving and Dave and Jeff are watching the pond with care when a bird suddenly zooms by near the car: "Black Swift!" Dave hollers and I swerve off the highway to the shoulder (mostly) and see the hefty dark swifts (there were at least two) swoosh by over the edge of the pond. An amazing break, a bird that we had only a slight chance at. 151. But there are no kingfishers over the Long Tom and no miraculous flocks of, say, flamingos coming off the lake.

8:30 Back to Royal Avenue for the dusk walk that might, conceivably, offer enough owl action to get us to the record. As we drive down Fir Butte Road we gaze at the wires in the gathering dimness, hoping for a waxwing. Dave suddenly points to a wire. Two birds. One is a Western Kingbird (already seen), one is ... a Western Bluebird! We are suddenly at 152, which means that it only takes one (owl, or anything else) to tie and two to beat the record. Those are not bad odds in western Oregon in, say, late March or early April, when owls are still territorial and responsive to hooting. In mid-May?

Western Screech-Owls. Ramiel Papish

Much harder when we've already checked our hypothetical Barn Owl site and had no owls.

So at dusk we walk out Royal Avenue as rails call and ducks zoom overhead. Canada Geese are sailing in for the evening and all manner of mammals are slithering through the water. At the end of Royal an American Wigeon suddenly calls. If we'd missed that and had, say, Gadwall at Stewart Pond we'd be dancing now. As it is, the wigeon's two-note whine seems to say, "next time, next time!" as darkness settles.

We walk back to the car having seen no owls over the marshes. We hope that the drier eastern fringe of the marsh will offer more chance of success. As we approach the car at 9:10 p.m., contemplating coming up with 152 when the record is 153, two dim forms sail over in close succession. The Night Masters: Great Horned Owls ! We have tied the record at 153.

10:00 Tying a record is far different from coming up short by one. There is an imperative to get that one more species. We have been birding for nineteen hours. We stagger to one possible site for Western Screech-Owl. Nothing. We agree to try one more spot that Dave thinks might be good. It is the boat landing at the bottom of River Loop 2 off north River Road. We get there at 10:10 p.m. We open the doors. Jeff says, "We're done" almost before the sound registers. Without any imitations, fake mouse noises, or other attempts to lure one in, a Western Screech-Owl is calmly hooting away right by the parking lot: "Go ho ho ho ho ho ho home." 154.

The late migration and cold-weather spring hurt us by keeping some species back from their usual migration times. Species that should have been fairly easy to find in an entire day in the field were not found: Nashville Warbler, Hermit Warbler, Lazuli Bunting, and Olive-sided Flycatcher were all missed. Some others (Hammond's Flycatcher, Pacific-slope Flycatcher, Warbling Vireo, Cassin's Vireo, Black-headed Grosbeak, and Swainson's Thrush) were in numbers much lower than the date would suggest.

Some small birds were missed for no particular reason: we never found a Kingfisher, our worst miss. We tried several places for Dipper: zilch. Pileated Woodpecker was not found, nor were Gray Jay or Townsend's Warbler, all of which were expected.

Among water birds and other larger species missed, Hooded Merganser, Red-shouldered Hawk, Peregrine Falcon, both grouse,

Mountain Quail, Black Turnstone, and Surfbird, Dunlin, Long-billed Dowitcher, snipe, Red-necked Phalarope, and Barn Owl are not rare (some breed) and we should do better on them in the future.

We did better on gulls than we might have, and coastal shorebirds were not bad for the mediocre Siuslaw estuary. The cool spring may have held back enough Golden-crowned Sparrows and Lincoln's Sparrows to keep us from finding them. Getting *just enough* of coastal birds such as alcids kept us alive. Likewise, one Downy Woodpecker, one Wrentit (a good twenty miles inland), and one Red-breasted Nuthatch suggest that we were pretty close to the edge.

As I wrote this account just after the event, I realized that we mistakenly marked Cedar Waxwing on the list even though my blurry mind does not recall that we ever found one. So in fact we tied the record after all, and we'll have to break it another time. It's a good incentive. We raised about three thousand dollars for the UO Museum.

I had made a couple of previous Big Day runs to eastern Oregon. I don't do them anymore, though record-setting runs close to 220 species have been made by others in the 2000s. There are other ways to combine birding with useful contributions to knowledge, as suggested by this entry from my journal, which came from the same atlasing project as the Burnt River Valley trip:

July 4, 1996

The United States is 220 years old today. I celebrated by getting up at 4 a.m. and driving to Greenleaf, Lane County Coast Range, where I arrived about 6:30 and began a morning of work in Oregon Breeding Bird Atlas cell number 27178. By 10:00 when I departed for Bandon I had found fifty species in twenty-six road miles, not bad for the Coast Range in July. Lake Creek and the upper Siuslaw River add much to the variety of the cell. Seventeen of the fifty had not been found in the cell in the previous year. From the look of the maps that Paul Adamus sent me, previous coverage had been in higher-elevation forest lands, so I stayed in the valleys.

The most unexpected bird was a Dusky Flycatcher seen and heard in an alder stand halfway between Indiola and Deadwood. There was also a Hammond's Flycatcher farther east. Other noteworthy and pleasant finds were broods of Common Merganser and Pileated Woodpecker, a small colony of Violet-green Swallows using a cliff face just east of Swisshome, several pair of Evening Grosbeaks, and a young Swainson's Thrush. Also an immature Gray Jay.

The swallows are among relatively few that we see in western Oregon using "natural" habitats; these are so much a town swallow west of the Cascades that seeing a colony using cliff nests seems strange, though of course they do this commonly in eastern Oregon.

The commonest singing birds in the valley were Warbling Vireo, Song Sparrow, Robin, Tree Swallow, Barn Swallow. There were many Willow Flycatchers (perhaps thirty all told), lots of Westerns, too. Wilson's Warblers and Swainson's Thrushes were fairly common. No doubt if I had been there at 5:30 I would have noted more thrushes. Several pairs of Cedar Waxwings and a number of Black-headed Grosbeaks, also.

In unexpectedly low numbers were Bewick's Wren (one), Winter Wren (two), Spotted Towhee (two), Chestnut-backed Chickadees (one), Steller's Jays (two), Band-tailed Pigeons (one), and Downy Woodpecker (one). I missed sapsucker, Hairy Woodpecker, Hermit Warbler, Wrentit, and other species that were no doubt present.

Atlasing projects have been a part of birding for a long time. They provide an opportunity to get into places we would not normally go, get away from pure listing, and perhaps spend time with people we don't usually bird with.

1999: California Gulch

On our 1994 trip to Arizona I missed several birds, including Montezuma Quail, Mexican Chickadee, Five-striped Sparrow, Scaled Quail, and Olive Warbler. I took another short trip with Rich Hoyer before the American Birding Association convention in Tucson in 1999. Among other things, we returned to the scene of the Situation in 1994, where a rare White Ibis of which we had heard rumors suddenly showed itself. But the real work was ahead—drive-up rarities are just not quite to Rich's taste.

When Rich says we need to be there at dawn, he really means dawn. And "there" is over two hours away. In the first gray pre-dawn gloaming I can finally see well enough to know that he has gone crazy.

He is driving his small pickup down what appears to be a mountain goat trail, except that mountain goats would not walk on such a mass of loose, broken rocks. I detected a civilized parking area a couple of miles back, yet we parketh not. This fanatical extension of our drive would not disturb me, being completely in character for Rich, except that I am inside the vehicle while he is doing this.

California Gulch lies right on the Mexican border south of Tucson. It has all the desert birds one would expect. It also has a small breeding population of Five-striped Sparrows. Rich told me that I needed to see Five-striped Sparrows. I believed him. Actually I had wanted to see them. Sort of. I had never seen them so I *should* want to see them, right? That is what birders do, right?

Another piece of rock spun off into the darkness as we bounced and shuddered up the last turn and suddenly parked in what Rich was obviously treating as a parking area. In the dimness it looked to me like a grove of junipers, but they are actually small oaks. By Arizona standards it was cool and pleasant when we got out of the car. Ahead of us was a trail that dropped into darkness: the sun was nowhere near up and we were on a low ridge above a dim chasm, the other side of which was walled by a ridge about the height of ours. Oh, yeah. It's called California *Gulch*. I get it. I got the Indulgent Look from Rich—I know it well, having known him for twenty years. We started down the trail.

The Five-striped Sparrow is a sparrow, and I am very fond of sparrows as a family. I have always enjoyed watching such species as Lincoln's Sparrow and Black-throated Sparrow, and my first views of Baird's Sparrow and LeConte's Sparrow will always stay with me. In the hour following our arrival I saw five different singing Five-striped Sparrows, most of them quite well. They are visually somewhat similar to a Black-throated Sparrow, with a more variegated head pattern and less black below.

As is true of many birds, seeing them in their natural habitat—the open shrub cover of a desert canyon wall at the break of dawn—is what made them especially memorable. It is not just seeing a species in isolation that makes the experience stand out, it is the entire context of the occasion. The hours of darkness, the hellish road (on the way out Rich actually had to stop and arrange some rocks to drive over), the predawn awakening of the desert with a hundred sounds.

That day we stayed in the canyon for several hours. In addition to the sparrows we saw Black-tailed Gnatcatchers, Varied Bunting, and a vocal Gray Hawk. As we walked unhurriedly back toward the trail out of the gulch, three nervous-looking Mexicans walked by going the other way. With our binoculars and alert demeanor we must have looked like border patrol outriders, for they gave us half-hearted smiles and said, "*No trabajo*" a couple of times, meaning that they had not been working in the U.S. Rich waved his binoculars and said something about *pajaros*, at which they perked up and relaxed a bit. Bird-watchers, for heavens sake. Who would have thought it?

Shortly after that we ran into Chris Benesh, an Arizona bird-tour guide with a small entourage of *ornituristas* looking for the sparrows. As we reached the car the morning was well along and quite warm already. And that oak grove was stuffed with cars, so apparently it was a parking lot after all. Then, to my astonishment, a string of teenagers appeared out of nowhere *on foot*, rather dusty and carrying binoculars, but looking very, very determined. Michael Retter from Illinois and Vjera Arnold, a friend from Oregon, had *walked in* all the way from the first parking area, a couple of miles over the rocks and dust, in the sunny morning, in the hope of seeing a Five-striped Sparrow. They managed to find exactly one, and watched it from some distance away.

So perhaps getting up at 3:00 a.m. had been a good idea after all.

On the way out, back on the "main" road, we stopped to check a promising hillside for Montezuma Quail, which I had never seen. I had heard them. Now I heard one again, somewhere up the steep, ticky, grassy, shrubby, rocky, no doubt snake-infested hillside. Rich and I worked our way up. We could hear the bird, but it was very hard to locate. Finally, after he was high on the hill and I was halfway up, sweating and swatting bugs, the quail emerged not twenty feet from my right foot, showed itself gloriously, then started walking downhill, invisible. A male "zumi" quail, as Michael and Vjera (today Vjera Thompson, having married her friend Eddie, whom she judged could be made into a birder) call them, is a visually unlikely object. Imagine a canteloupe with legs, jam a tennis ball onto the top at one end, and then dip the resulting aerodynamically unsound spheroid into the machine that makes caramel swirl ice cream, and there you have it. A prototype, perhaps. The reality is an astonishing symphony in ochre, cinnamon, and maple sugar, one of the most stunning birds I have ever seen.

Just at that moment, as the quail ambled downhill in tall grass, the carload of teen wolves, including Michael and Vjera, rolled up and stopped at the sight of our car.

"What do you have?" they hollered up the hill.

"Montezuma Quail walking downhill right toward you!"

They burst from the car, trying to remain quiet, and just as they had binoculars at the ready, the "zumi" quail walked out to the edge of the bluff, looked at them and strolled laterally away from them, affording great views.

They had missed it until that moment. They hadn't seen it—*yet*.

2000: Everything's Big in Texas

My long-anticipated Texas trip combined a personal five-day trip with Rich Hoyer and a WINGS guided birding tour for which Rich was co-leader with Jon Dunn. I was in Texas from April 10 to 22, 2000, but there was always a sense of being in an old-West sort of place, where anything could happen and probably had. Pioneer ornithologist Florence Merriam Bailey wrote thus of her visit there:

Before sundown we passed our next landmark, Santa Rosa Ranch—the names marking the road between Corpus Christi and Brownsville are those of ranches, windmills, or motts ["the local name for a small grove on the open prairie," she defines elsewhere]—and after driving up to the [wagon] hubs through freshet lakes we camped for the night between two runs, much to the dissatisfaction of the old Texas camp man who said that he had been caught that way in winter, camping beside a dry wash and having to stand up to his knees in water half the night! The only excitements of the night, however, proved to be the passing of birds in the darkness, the fine chip of small migrants, the squawk of Black-crowned Night Herons, and low over us the thrilling swishing of heavy wings, probably those of Wild Turkeys.

[Another day] At last the low line of trees we had been wearily traveling toward for hours was reached and proved a veritable oasis

in the sand belt. An oak mott, San Ignatia by name, raised only a
few feet above the general level but made up of large old live oaks
that dispensed cool shade through the hot hours and offered shelter
to birds from all the region round about. When the aviary had
settled down for the night a rattlesnake, discovered too near our
tent, had to be shot, and at the report of the gun an amazingly large
flock of Scissor-tails burst out of the tree, proving what the oak mott
meant on the treeless prairie.

Florence Merriam Bailey, 1900, as quoted in *No Woman*
Tenderfoot: Florence Merriam Bailey, Pioneer Naturalist, Harriet
Kofalk, 1989

It is said that everything is big in Texas. Having seen the
comprehensive ugliness of Houston poured across the landscape both
from the air and now from the ground, waiting for Rich at the car
rental place, I had no reason to doubt that at least the more crude
aspects of Texas were as large as anyone could possibly conceive. When
Rich got there, he discovered that we had been assigned something in
the sports car line rather than the sedate sedans that I usually get. It
was even bright red. We were in a what-the-heck mood, so signed for
it and resolved to leave Houston behind as soon as possible.

Leaving Houston behind is rather like leaving the Internal Revenue
Service behind. You can talk about it. You can even choreograph it
and execute the steps after a fashion. Yet when you have done all
of that, rented the car, checked the map, aimed west, and driven on
and on, there is ultimately still Houston there grasping for you with
moist, adhesive fingers. Keeping our eyes resolutely on our goal some
hours to the west, we eventually fought free of the last tendrils of this
Gorgon of the Gulf. Ahead lay the hill country and freedom.

One of the birds that most of us fantasize about from time to time
is that stunning particle of spun sunlight and ebony, the Golden-
cheeked Warbler. I had certainly fantasized about it many times, and
an Oregonian has a right to fantasize with some technical credibility:
one of North America's wildest off-course vagrants was the Golden-
cheeked Warbler that somehow reached the banding station on the
Farallon Islands off San Francisco on September 9, 1971. The only
other vagrant was in Florida, of all places. It happens. It could happen
to *me*. But the best way to see these birds is to go where they belong,
to see where and how they make a living. And with this in mind we

Birds of Laguna Atascosa. Ramiel Papish

had left the Gorgon behind and were heading for the central Texas hill country. It was dark by the time we got to our motel in Kerrville.

The Texas hill country is often written Hill Country, and with good reason. This part of Texas is capital indeed, consisting of the whole eastern slab of the Edwards Plateau, which rises above the panting lowlands and offers a truly exceptional variety of bird life. For this is one of the most vivid east-meets-west zones on the continent. Many species common to the eastern and gulf avifauna reach the plateau via its riparian valleys, and in some cases reach the edge of their range here. From the west the desert fauna moves across the drier top of the plateau, extending farther east here than anywhere else in the south-central U.S.

Into this seething blend zone, full of possibility and several kinds of ticks, we went the next morning. Our destination was Lost Maples State Park, an oddly named recreation area on the edge of the plateau. In considering the peculiar name, one thinks of such venues as the San Francisco Cow Palace or the Cambridge Corn Exchange in England (in which I once attended a concert)—the question is not where the name comes from, but why it persists: these maples were obviously found some time ago. I concede that "Lost Maples" does have a certain come-hither cachet that no doubt plays better among the *turistas* than, say, George W. Bush Memorial Hillside.

Our first experience at Lost Maples was sobering: we heard a distant Golden-cheeked Warbler, neither heard nor saw any Black-capped Vireos, our other desired bird here, and found not much activity. Things improved a bit as we walked up one of the trails that led to a small impoundment along the creek. We heard a warbler near the river and went down to the edge of a low bluff to look for it. Suddenly it was right in front of us, moving from right to left, even singing occasionally.

I had always imagined a Golden-cheeked Warbler as looking more or less like a Townsend's, which we see a lot in Oregon. Not so. It is superficially similar, but the sheer blackness of much of the feathering gives it a far more formal, no-nonsense look compared to similar *Dendroica*, much as a priest with a simple collar becomes a completely different kind of being in high drag for Mass. This was a bird I had never really expected to see (after all, I never expected to be able to visit Texas when I was a kid birder looking at these delights in my Peterson guide), yet here it was, right where it was supposed to be.

As an added bonus, there was a Green Kingfisher just up the trail at the impoundment. This is about as far north as they get, and we had not really expected one here, so the chance to see this diminutive diver lurking on its low stick perches or darting across the stream was a special delight.

We did not find any Black-capped Vireos at Lost Maples, so we tried for them a little farther south at Neal's Lodge resort, where Rich had permission to enter the lodge property to seek them. It was well that he did, for a pair was breeding right behind the buildings. They moved in a wide circle, so if we stayed in one place each bird would eventually cross in front of us, singing and showing its strange dipped-in-licorice plumage.

We headed south into the increasingly flat, hot world of the Rio Grande Valley. Scissor-tailed Flycatchers and, curiously, Golden-fronted Woodpeckers, were the common "highway" birds, the woodpeckers new to me and using far smaller trees for feeding than I would have thought possible for a fairly hefty picid. I soon saw my first Crested Caracara, a strange concept with wings. By evening we had reached Zapata, on the Rio Grande River.

The Valley

Certain places acquire a name that remains both instantly meaningful yet devoid of sufficient visible linguistic hooks upon which that apparent meaning can be hung. When I worked as a lobbyist around the state capitol building in Salem, Oregon, I learned that the capitol itself was simply called The Building. People would say "She's over in The Building," and everyone knew which building was meant. The capitol letters, if you will, were universally inferred.

At Malheur National Wildlife Refuge, where I have spent so many years birding, there are several hedges, speaking in the horticultural sense, yet only one Hedge. Anyone with any experience there who says "it flew into The Hedge" only means the lilac hedge at the northeastern edge of the complex. No other hedge is ever meant. The other nominal hedges around the headquarters buildings must content themselves to remain forever lower-case, dependent on the fickle attachments of adjectives and boorish neighboring nouns: a phrase like "the dense green hedge south of the office" denies a hedge much chance to shine.

Such is The Valley. There are many valleys in Texas, some of which are quite substantial and have names in common usage, for example the Red River Valley, but a Texan who says "I was in the valley" means only The Valley: the immensely long, surprisingly shallow controlled meander of the Rio Grande that separates south Texas from Mexico politically if not culturally.

We birded in the valley the next day. I do not like hot climates and the lure of tropical birding has never been clamped between my lips no matter how seductively cast. Nonetheless, I wanted to see some of the birds to be found in south Texas, and Rich, a professional bird guide after all, seemed to know where they all were. We wandered around a city park which seemed to contain just one White-collared Seedeater—is this specific bird the one that *all* birders add to their lists?

We handed a somewhat casual fee to a jolly private park overseer in order to gaze upon Brown Jays hogging a feeder, more mapgie than jay. I suspect that the casualness of the fee had a direct relationship to the jolliness of the staff. While I was watching my first Ringed Kingfisher, quite a robust creature compared to the standard Belted Kingfishes found in most of North America, a Muscovy Duck flapped over in its curiously Jurassic manner, while Green Jays crept through the denser riverside yards, emerging into the sun just long enough for their electrifying green, blue, and yellow plumage to recharge before returning to guard their arboreal keeps.

As we worked our way down the valley we had extraordinary success: Kiskadees displaying kingfisher envy, an incongruous Broad-winged Hawk passing over, Audubon's Oriole whispering its apologetic song, Gray Hawk watching a Mexican birthday party aross the river (why are trees in Mexico painted white?), Tropical Parula where it was supposed to be, Pauraques emerging with churring anticipation in the twilight, and finally a distant view of a Hook-billed Kite flopping about over Santa Ana, proving by its impossibly nonchalant wingbeats that antigravity is possible. Although the Gray-crowned Yellowthroat that we saw at Santa Ana was the "best" bird we saw in the valley, and a true rarity by American Birding Association standards, my memories of that entire region are dominated by a snake.

I am usually snake-neutral. Some people loathe snakes, but I do not have an innate revulsion except for spiders. Some people are fascinated by snakes, seek them out and know them well, e.g., Rich Hoyer. His father is a noted expert on rubber boas and he was raised with snakes. I on the other hand came to know them in mid-life when I worked as a lobbyist. I always enjoy seeing snakes and have even enjoyed watching rattlesnakes from a safe distance in the wild.

As we were about to leave the Sabal Palm Grove sanctuary in extreme south Texas, I noticed a strange snake that I called to Rich's attention. It was medium sized and quite languid in movements, a stunning patterned blue and green in color. It was a speckled racer, *Drymobius margaritiferus*, which Rich would rename pearled racer if he could. It occurs only in that one area in the entire U.S., and seeing one is not an everyday thing.

The upper coast

There have been so many chronicles of the Texas coast, High Island, and so on that I don't want to simply repeat them with gasps of awe.

The area is a superb place to look for and at birds, and the week I spent on the WINGS tour in April 2000 was extremely enjoyable and allowed me to see, in combination with the earlier days with Rich, some fifty-three life birds, the last time I could get even half that number in North America.

A few experiences stand out. The special conditions faced by trans-gulf migrants are hard to describe but the visual images from time in the field can be quite memorable. For example, one day as we were driving along the outer beach near High Island, with no vegetation nearby but grass, we noticed a small bird on the fence wire. It proved to be as unlikely a beach wire-sitter as we could imagine: a Black-throated Green Warbler. It must have been able to see the tree line a mile or so to the north; it was too tired to get there.

At High Island there is a set of bleachers where birders can sit to watch the waterhole where migrants come to drink. The flow of birds in and out of the waterhole is impressive, but sometimes a particular juxtaposition is so exceptional as to re-fry an observer's optical credulity. That moment came for me when, for some reason, a male Indigo Bunting, Painted Bunting, Brown Thrasher, and Golden-winged Warbler lined up next to each other to drink. My color-processing center seemed to suffer a temporary short and after a moment I simply lowered my binoculars. What can one say in the face of such glory?

2000: The Importance of "Yet"

In 1967, we left our boy, with no knowledge of first state records, sliding down the dunes. Now the circle closes, for he is back on the coast. On September 24, 2000, I was birding with Hendrik Herlyn and Luke Bloch near Florence, Oregon, checking our usual spots. In the morning we decided to walk out the Siltcoos River trail to the ocean and check for shorebirds in the small but productive backwater pond just inside the low dunes. This is an attractive walk almost any time of year, though the beach end of it is closed in summer owing to the presence of several pairs of Snowy Plovers, which are very rare now on the Oregon coast.

The Siltcoos River has one of the least impressive estuaries on the Oregon coast. Is there a definitive definition of estuary? My dictionary simply describes it with Whitmanesque directness as where the river meets the sea. Well, fair enough, but what if the river is only fifteen inches deep and as many feet wide?   The Siltcoos does display characteristics of larger estuaries in that its lower reaches are tidal, with salt water moving in and out and the sand and mud susceptible to subtle shifts and revisions.

In fact, the Siltcoos has one distinction that makes it one of the most interesting coastal streams. Its outfall runs through shallow sand dunes and flats for the last hundred yards or so before it reaches the ocean, and the combination of low flow volume, winter storms, high tides, and wind causes the configuration of the outfall to vary widely from year to year. The entire lower part of the river, including the location at which it reaches the sea, has shifted radically from north to south, adding and subtracting serpentine bends, several times in the twenty years I have been going there.

Some astonishing birds have occurred along this unassuming patch of water and its appendage ponds and backwaters. Oregon's first Eastern Yellow Wagtail was found here. Ruff, Curlew Sandpiper, and other unusual shorebirds have been seen in this limited piece of habitat. Steve Heinl and I once saw a Stilt Sandpiper that flew in, stayed about two minutes, and flew away, never to be seen again. But more than its potential for exotica, the lower Siltcoos has a certain charisma not found at the larger river mouths in Oregon.

First of all, although it gets *turista* traffic, especially in summer and early fall, it has a certain primal aspect, its marshy banks guarded by lichen-heavy pines and dense huckleberry and salal, its waters inhabited by otters, mergansers, and red-legged frogs, its mouth supporting one of Oregon's only coastal colonies of Snowy Plovers. It is also so narrow and shallow that its only boat traffic consists of canoes and kayaks (not allowed to touch the shore during plover breeding season). In the off-season or on a rainy day, it is possible to walk its sandy mouth without seeing any other person—a rare experience on Oregon's sand beaches.

At many points along the river trail, it is possible to find a gap in the shrubbery and perch on or above the bank, just watching to see what goes by. Merlins perch on the snags and hunt the meadow. A kingfisher is always arguing about something on its way up and down the channel. The local Wrentits have become accustomed to people owing to the adjacent campground and creep through the huckleberry stands to peer at intruders: their desiccated churring seems to say "more of them... ... more of them" to each other.

When birding the Siltcoos we always reach the outer sands with a certain anticipation. After all, this is where the wagtail was found, and anything could be there. One year a dark, medium-sized swift went tearing by us—in mid-October. We had such brief looks that we could never be sure, but it may well have been Oregon's first Chimney Swift—one that got away. Hendrik Herlyn saw a Curlew Sandpiper here once; it instantly fled with its escort of Pectorals, only to appear at Coos Bay the next day for a leisurely stroll in front of video cameras.

Will we finally find a Red-throated Pipit there? How about a nice pratincole? As I mentioned earlier, the most important word in birding is "yet." It has not come by *yet*. It was here but flew away and has not come back *yet*. We have not found it *yet*. The Siltcoos is a "yet" kind of place.

Yet was on our minds on September 24, 2000. We did not find much in the way of shorebirds, but as we stood looking at the large but undistinguished early-season gull flock, mostly Californias and Westerns with a few Heermann's, at the mouth of the shallow river, a small bird came apparently from nowhere—probably down from the sky over the ocean—and landed on the sand near some clumps of beach grass. A quick look showed it to be not the hoped-for exotic pipit (Oregon did not have its first confirmed Red-throated Pipit until 2003) but some kind of finchy thing that quickly resolved into a longspur.

But it was not the expected Lapland Longspur, which normally passes along the outer coast of Oregon in small numbers from late September through October. It was far too buffy underneath. It flew a short distance, offered some tail views while preening and then flew off above an area of deeper grass, which it may or may not have entered.

As we compared notes at the time and during the day, it became obvious that the bird did not have the heavy rufous wing edgings of a Lapland, nor was the face pattern or tail pattern, showing limited white on only two outer feathers, quite right. But all of these marks *were* right for another species that had not been on our minds at all: Smith's Longspur!   Despite our rather brief views we concluded after checking several references that this is what we'd found. It was a first Oregon record. It was never seen again. Not until October, 2003 did

Oregon's second record occur, and this time it was photographed. The jinx was broken!

"Sort of like a meadowlark..."

Later in the day we met Eugene birder Don DeWitt, a retired high school teacher whom I had known for many years, along the south jetty road near Florence. At his suggestion, we decided, despite the midday heat, not uncommon on the outer coast in fall, to walk out the principal transverse dike leading from the road into the deflation plain that lies east of the road. This dike passes through clumps of willows and eventually reaches a series of small ponds that are often worth checking for shorebirds. The general area has contained such delights as Sharp-tailed Sandpiper, Ruff, Buff-breasted Sandpiper, Hudsonian Godwit, and other unusual species over the years. But none of those prepared us for what was waiting out on the dry sand.

We walked all the way out the dike, finding little but a remarkably unwary White-fronted Goose and a flock of goldfinches. Birders never use the word "tame" to describe an approachable bird, of course, since a tame bird might conceivably be an escape and therefore uncountable. Thus all approachable birds are "unwary," which is perfectly acceptable.

We pursued an unknown pipit to a small pond to the south of the dike, where it became an American Pipit of the standard North American flavor, sometimes called Buff-bellied Pipit. We then decided to conduct the usual "death march" on the dry sand flats, looking mainly for pipits or longspurs. We spread out into a skirmish line to make sure nothing went unflushed and walked northward.

About two hundred yards north of the dike we noticed movement that proved to be an American Golden-Plover. Golden-plovers are expected in this area, but are by no means seen every visit. We had seen two Pacific Golden-Plovers at the jetty a couple of hours earlier, so our "dessert" after the longspur was already quite fulfilling. Near the golden-plover, a second bird caught our attention with its huge pale golden supercilium as it ducked through a small patch of spike-rush. The bird was obviously a plover, based on its shape, size, bill shape, and behavior. While the wide eyeline and posture superficially evoked the image of a Western Meadowlark (which occurs in the same habitat), a closer examination of the bird's structure immediately revealed its shorebird nature.

It was not a Buff-breasted Sandpiper, which sometimes occurs there in fall. The bold eye line and black and golden back pattern ruled out all of the smaller *Charadrius* species as well as Mountain Plover, Killdeer, and the rare vagrant Lesser Sand-Plover.   But it had gone into the rush patch without showing its front and had not yet emerged.

Was it a strange *Pluvialis* plover? Black-bellied Plover was easily ruled out as it never shows the amount of bright buff and gold on back, wings, and especially supercilium. The three species of golden-plovers differ in size and shape of their supercilium and back and wing pattern (which is more spangled, consisting of smaller golden spots and irregular edgings to the coverts and tertials, rather than the bold golden edging around dark feather centers displayed by our bird before it disappeared). So what was it?

When it emerged, it showed us its breast, which looked just the way it was supposed to—a pale transverse band across a grayish-tan field—but that species had never occurred here! It offered a variety of excellent views and to our elation was the bird that we had fantasized about for many years *in this exact location*: a *Eurasian Dotterel*—Oregon's first record and one of fewer than ten records *anywhere* south of Alaska.

Eurasian Dotterel. Photo by Eric Horvath.

We had found two first state records in less than six hours, in places we each had birded dozens of times before. Such is the joy of birding.

That's when I discovered that I had left my cell phone a half-mile back in the car, so I moved at top lumber through the sand back to and along the dike, all the way to the car to call the bird in to the rare bird alert network.

I never saw it again.

2003: Just a Long Weekend

In May 2003 I returned to Arizona with my friend Daniel Farrar to look for a couple of birds I had never seen and to give Daniel his first Arizona experience. We left Eugene on Friday morning and returned on Monday evening. Rich Hoyer was our guide, as usual, and provider of great food. We had a remarkably successful trip, and Daniel, who had hoped for forty lifers, ended up seeing fifty-seven.

French Joe Canyon

You call this a road? OK, it shows signs of having been designed as a road, which cannot be said of the route into California Gulch, which a mule would reject as unfeasible. Rich has driven the Miller Canyon road many times. One advantage of traveling with a professional guide is that the sound of my head banging against the doorframe and roof with accompanying rodentlike squeals does not distract him at all from getting us to the trailhead.

Why did we want to get to the trailhead so early on a day meant for sleeping in? Well, we don't have to think about that because when birding with Rich you are going to be there at dawn, so get used to it. Daniel and I had arrived the day before (it hardly seemed possible) from Oregon. After an afternoon on the west side of the Chiricahuas and a fortuitous picnic site that turned out to be underneath a Mexican Chickadee nest hole, we had gone to bed thinking of Rufous-capped Warblers. That was our primary goal on the trail up French Joe Canyon.

Having filed the car in a shady spot, we started walking up the trail, which turned out to be quite a variable track. Sometimes a well-marked trail, sometimes an open space under a sycamore stand, sometimes what looked and felt suspiciously like a stream bed ("It's the trail. Come on!" was Rich's commonest statement). I said nothing—well, nothing he could hear—when the "trail" stopped, starting again three feet higher over a well-polished rock shelf.

Partway up the canyon, we heard a calling Montezuma Quail from a grassy hillside to the south. A very steep, rather rocky grassy hillside, of course. Directly up which Rich and Daniel immediately went. I had seen Montezuma Quail once before, but eventually heaved myself up the hill after them, wondering how many species of tick occur in Arizona and what kind of venomous snakes prefer steep, rocky, grassy hillsides.

One of the *other* advantages of hiring Rich as a guide is that he can imitate both sexes of Montezuma Quail perfectly, and there is nothing more interesting to a male zumi quail far up an unscalable hillside than a female zumi quail calling from the bottom of said hillside. And down it came. These quail do nothing in a hurry, but with deliberate purpose it walked straight down the hillside until we could see the grass moving. Then its head. Then the top of it. Then Daniel could see almost all of his first zumi quail standing just up the hill from us, casting about this way and that while uttering a doubtful hoarse "freeeuw" and no doubt wondering whether six-foot-three Rich was really the mate he had in mind.

After the great quail-call counterpoint, we went on up the canyon until we reached a fairly narrow section with dense shrubbery and small side fissures. At first we found only a few of the commoner birds, then Rich heard a Rufous-capped Warbler just down the hill. We scrambled down to the area and saw ... nothing. But we could still hear strange call notes and there were furtive movements behind the wall of dense shrubbery. Suddenly a wrenlike bird zipped across the draw and disappeared into one of the small rifts. Shortly thereafter it emerged, and a second bird followed it.

A Rufous-capped Warbler is not the kind of bird you'd expect a warbler to be if you are used to seeing warbler migrations at High Island, Texas, Crane Creek, Ohio, or Cape May. Although bright yellow underneath with a rufous cap, it can be hard to see as it leaps and flits in and out of desert shrubbery. Wrenlike in appearance and to some extent in behavior, it is quite active. We were able to watch two of them for about twenty minutes.

Montezuma Quail. Ramiel Papish

As we walked out (crawling down the stone waterfall on the "trail") we met another group of birders just below Quail Hill. We mentioned that we'd seen the quail up there, and they went off after it. That poor quail was destined once again for disappointment in love.

Miller Canyon

Why do interesting birds all live at the top of steep hills? It is true that some wonderful birds can be seen from a reclining chair near, say, the hummingbird feeders at the Beatty's in Miller Canyon or at Mary Jo Ballator's Ash Canyon B&B south of Sierra Vista, but Rich told me that I was going to walk up the gently sloping canyon trail and have a pleasant morning watching a Flame-colored Tanager. I have known Rich for many years and I know better than to believe that he uses the phrase "gentle slope" to mean the same thing I do, so I knew I was in for a haul. It was worse than I imagined after the relatively easy first half-mile. Up, up, and more up, made worse by the loose rocky surface.

In my pre-diet phase I was lugging 240 pounds of, uh, muscle up that hill, and after half an hour of gasping, sweating, step after step, it occurred to me that I had no obligation to see a Flame-colored Tanager. I could stop right now and watch a Red-faced Warbler. A Painted Redstart. Lovely birds that I can't see too often. Why, exactly, did I need to see that tanager? Rich is the only person I know who can combine a look of indulgence with a superior glower. I hasten to say that he reserves this look for old friends and I have never seen it on his WINGS tours. I kept climbing. After a while the physical aspects became a genuine problem and I could only move about ten feet before stopping.

Up, up, ever up. And then of all things we found people. Other birders. Standing along the trail where the tanager should have been. But was not. I staggered up a little more, since the trail was slightly more level here. There were not many birds. Rich and Daniel were trying to get a good look at a Greater Pewee that had perched so that it was in line with the sun no matter where an observer stood, a skill I had noticed before in that species.

We waited. A couple of Western Tanagers wandered through. Suddenly someone we had not seen before came dashing *down* the trail: there were more birders *above* us, it seemed. And they had just seen the tanager. They thought. But it had disappeared. So most of us heaved ourselves farther up the canyon, close now to the saddle. Rich stayed below for a while, and we exchanged non-sightings via our FRS radios. Eventually Rich came up and worked his way across the little canyon, finding nothing.

How thick a layer does congealed sweat actually make? It was not falling off in slabs, but the rest and attendant cooling cycle had left me feeling ready to be sprinkled with minced filberts, carved, and served with a nice Umpqua Valley riesling, and there was *no tanager*.

We moved a short distance back down the trail. Unlike my experience in 1994 above Madera Canyon in June, Miller Canyon in early May 2003 contained relatively few birds, mostly spread out. A few Plumbeous Vireos were worth studying, as we occasionally get reports of them in southeastern Oregon, and Daniel and I had little experience with them. Their songs sometimes aborted on takeoff and then picked up again, unlike the Cassin's Vireos to which we were accustomed, and these sharply separated burry phrases sounded rather like a distant *Myiarchus* flycatcher, an impression that I have never had with Cassin's or Blue-headed Vireos. At that point I was thinking that the chance to hear and see these plain, vocal vireos was a good consolation prize, but one we could have awarded ourselves a mile farther downhill.

That is when word flashed up the trail. The Flame-colored Tanager had come in right over our heads but was *completely invisible* in the pines! Every birder convened where we were, all looking into the dimness above. Movement. A *Western* Tanager came into the open. It then flew out into a more open tree growing from lower in the canyon, ending up close to our eye level. And beside it there was suddenly an orange bird, a strangely bright bird, more oriole than tanager in color, and with a certain brawny bulk to it. From nowhere, it seemed, the Flame-colored Tanager had appeared right in front of us, and proceeded to move around from perch to perch offering every possible view.

I did not think it possible, but the trail down was even slower than the trail up, for gravity caused me to slip on every loose rock, with my half-strength right knee suddenly protesting. But for some reason I seemed to weigh nothing.

2003: Everything Flies in Alaska

In the late summer of 2002 I saw an ad for unusually low air fares from Oregon to Alaska. I started to think of ways to get to that state for some birding. I called Rich Hoyer and expounded some wild scheme in which he and I would immediately drop what we were doing and fly to Alaska. He used to work on the Pribilofs so he knows his way around at least part of the state.

I have known Rich for years, so even over the telephone I can see him rolling his eyes. After they'd rolled a couple of cycles and come to rest, I calmed down and we discussed ways to do an Alaska trip, tentatively scheduled for August of 2003. As winter came on, our original idea of just going up there had metamorphosed into the idea of a private tour through WINGS, in which we could include friends of ours who wanted to bird Alaska. We'd spend just a week, around Nome and at Gambell, and Rich would be able to earn a little as the guide and cook. Having Rich as our cook would give us a culinary advantage over all other tour groups, I reasoned, which proved to be the case in spectacular and unexpected ways.

After a few false starts and personnel changes, our group was assembled, paid for, and watching the calendar. I had conspired with the parents of Noah Strycker, a high school student who often birded with me, to send him on this trip as a graduation present. The rest of the group consisted of Dan and Anne Heyerly, Eugene birders whom I had known for years, Tom Nelson, a retired entomologist from Corvallis, and Portland birders Mark Miller, Marcia Marvin, and Al Murray.

It is one thing to know intellectually that travel in Alaska is mainly by air; it is something else to live the dream. Noah and I left Eugene about 9:30 a.m., changed planes in Seattle and again in Anchorage, and reached Nome about 8:30 p.m. Our first "birdable" view of Alaska was above the Arctic Circle at the Kotzebue airport, which consists of a runway built on a dike in the sound. We therefore had views of a few birds as we landed, sat on the runway, and took off. And ... there is a duck in that pond. It could be our first eider. It could be almost anything. Actually, it could even be an American Wigeon, of which we had each seen thousands. Well, we had to start our Alaska experience with something.

Nome

Standing in the jammed waiting room in Nome, I was feeling very comfortable, even in the crowd. Too comfortable. I had left my down-lined waterproof jacket on the plane! I shoved my way to the counter and asked about my coat. The counter person went out to the plane and returned with my coat. Northern Alaska in late August is moist and cool, at least it was in 2003. Without that coat, specifically acquired at an REI sale in February with this trip in mind, I would have been in trouble.

8:30 in Nome in late August is nowhere near sundown, so after offloading our gear at the Aurora Inn, we piled back into the van and took off down the road to Safety Sound, where we had a taste of Alaska in preparation for the next day. The following day was our one full-length "official" birding effort around Nome, as we would in theory leave for Gambell the following day—if the weather lifted.

The Teller Road goes northwest from Nome and climbs into a series of hills that seems to go on forever beyond the Snake River. Before we left the lowlands we stopped at a large stand of willows, where Rich hooted up several Gray-cheeked Thrushes. A Northern Waterthrush chinked loudly but would not emerge. We drove in and out of low clouds and mist in the hope of seeing ptarmigan cross the road or perch up like Chukars on some visible rock. They did not.

We did have a productive slog up a hill beyond the Penny River crossing. I was a bit to the left of the rest of the group, moving toward a small willow draw while the others went up toward a rocky hillside that seemed to hold promise of ptarmigan. Something moved. A flick of white in the willows? Or something larger far beyond on the hillside?

I used my FRS radio to point the rest of the group toward the lower hillside, where I thought I had seen a wheatear-like flit. I stayed down in the willows and suddenly saw that some of the leaves were moving. Hoary Redpolls were crawling about, picking for food. Then Rich called me: there *were* wheatears on the hillside. Tom had stayed back by the car owing to a bad knee, and when we got back he said that another Northern Wheatear had come right out by the road. All in all, a successful jaunt. But where were the ptarmigan?

One thing I had not expected was that the hillside tundra was not solid, even on fairly steep slopes. It was, rather, a dense spongy mat of several kinds of thick vegetation including big patches of a crisp and moist but essentially flavorless small berry; as I recall they are called crowberries. We tried them and concluded that they were better suited for crows. Walking on this surface was like walking across an ill-constructed dance floor, since it gave slightly—or substantially—in unpredictable directions.

On the way back down the hills, we stopped at the Penny River crossing, where an Arctic Warbler had been seen the day before. I managed to hear and see one right by the road, but apparently the sight of me convinced it to migrate that very minute, because it could not be found again. As we wandered about, a family of Harlequin Ducks floated down the river. We did not see much else, and did not feel like walking off too far into the dense willows, where bears were quite likely.

The road east to Safety Sound passes by a collection of placer mining claims that have various forms of shacks on them between the road and Norton Sound. These mini-habitats for people are made of wood, corrugated metal, and apparently whatever came to hand. Few seemed to be occupied. Along this stretch of road we at first found few birds, though there were little clusters of Gray-crowned Rosy-Finches here and there, including some that were hanging around a feeder in the loose cluster of homes called Nook.

Our first revelation along this road came with the realization that a large piece of driftwood sticking up out of the beach gravel was in fact half Gyrfalcon. Not only was its upper half a Gyrfalcon sitting potoo-like at the end of a snag, but it was a *white* Gyrfalcon, which none of us had seen or expected in western Alaska—they are more regular in eastern Canada and Greenland. There are few birds more visually impressive than a white Gyrfalcon, a massive, powerful raptor that flies with astonishing speed while seeming to flap its wings with only casual interest.

The second revelation had nothing to do with birds. We became aware as we drove down the edge of Safety Sound that there were short wooden tripods with central towers spaced more or less evenly for miles near the shore. In fact, we saw a Gyrfalcon on one on our return drive. These proved to be trail markers for the final stage of the Iditarod, surely the most insane and perhaps the toughest competitive race ever devised.

It is hard enough to imagine crossing Alaska at all, let alone by dogsled in mid-winter. Yet early biologists did so under conditions in which rescue was not even a possibility. One of the more entertaining political confrontations in recent years came when naturalist Mardy Murie, in her nineties, faced off at a meeting with Alaska Senator Ted Stevens and reminded him that she knew a bit about Alaska, since she had crossed the Brooks Range by sled on her honeymoon in *January 1925*, when Stevens was a not-yet-two-year-old child in subarctic Indiana. Murie lived to be 101. *Brava*.

The Alaska Airlines terminal has a framed photo of a dogsled coming around a bend. Only my third look revealed that it was a personalized copy, signed along the bottom by what I took to be the Iditarod winners or that year's finishers. I was looking at Susan Butcher's original signature, in Nome, with gyrfalcons not so far down the road. It was a long way in time and space from that first Audubon's Warbler in Margaret Markley's back yard in Eugene.

Beyond falconhurst, we finally started seeing some waterfowl, including both King and Common Eiders. Unfortunately we were here in August during the season when all eiders are a demure brown. Not until June 2007 in Barrow would I see them in their spring glory, but that is for another book. Toward the eastern end of the Safety Sound channel, we finally found a sizable flock of shorebirds, though we'd seen a Bar-tailed Godwit at the Nome River bridge earlier. The weather was cool and moist as we walked out to the low rise overlooking an area of wet grass and small channels. Dowitchers, Pectorals, and peeps dashed back and forth, often landing within or behind clumps of grass. Then something a little more colorful crept out in the open, though at a distance.

"Sharp-tailed Sandpiper" was Rich's matter-of-fact announcement. I had seen them twice before in Oregon, but most of those present had not seen them at all. There seemed to be two or perhaps three of these lovely peach-breasted shorebirds walking methodically about, largely in or immediately next to big patches of grass. That made them hard to see, but eventually everyone had a look at them.

We reached the Solomon bridge pretty pleased with our variety of birds, though numbers had generally been low. We stopped at the north end of the bridge to scan for whatever might be around. Almost immediately Rich and others heard a high-pitched sound that might have been a Red-throated Pipit. There were a few American Pipits flying around and landing on the rocks and dirt below the bridge abutments, but we saw no Red-throated Pipits. After a couple of minutes we heard the sound again and to our surprise we noted that one of the pipits closest to us right below the road had pale legs. And a heavily streaked back. And heavy streaks below. It was a Red-throated Pipit, one of at least three that proved to be in the area. We learned then and at Gambell that we could sometimes pick out the Red-throated from the American Pipits because they looked a little shorter-tailed in flight, more the shape of a finch or Savannah Sparrow than that of a pipit.

As we returned to Nome we suddenly came upon a herd of musk oxen. These immense motile mops added a curiously prehistoric air to the landscape as they slogged slowly along a small draw. It was not hard to imagine animals much like these walking back and forth to Asia when the Bering land bridge—no great way off—still existed.

The next morning we were scheduled to leave for Gambell, on St. Lawrence Island, at 9:30. However, the forty-five-minute Gambell flight can only be undertaken from Nome when visual conditions on the north point of the island allow landing. And at 9:30 they did not. Nor did they at 10:30. We kept running around Nome birding in between these false starts, but a little after 11:00, it looked like we might go. The tall woman in jeans and sweatshirt who had been checking items behind the counter suddenly emerged and said "All for Gambell," and we walked out onto the pavement where the Beechcraft King Air was waiting. This was easily the smallest plane I had ever been in, and as the woman checked us all off, we stuffed ourselves into the thinly padded seats, trying to decide how much clothing to keep on in the close confines of the cabin.

Then to our surprise the woman got on, edged between us to the front of the plane, sat down in the front left seat and started the engines. We were not familiar with the casual norms of arctic air travel, and had thought Jackie was the counter clerk. It turns out that she was from Iowa and had been flying for twenty years. Not only that, but she was a birder— her feeder had hosted a Bullfinch in Nome the previous winter.

The flight out was smooth, far quieter than I had expected, and rather featureless, since the cloud cover was pretty solid. The landing at Gambell was different than any I had previously experienced, since I could see out of the front of the plane as we dove right over the

Birds of Alaska. Ramiel Papish

village and the runway changed its angle to meet our soft touchdown. We were in Gambell, about which I had read for thirty years.

Gambell

How to describe Gambell? It is many things. First, a Yupik village that has been more or less at the same location for over three *thousand* years (there is evidence of hunting here from 1500 B.C.), thus matched in longevity in the Americas only by a very small number of fixed communities, mostly in Latin America. Today the village proper consists of about seven hundred people living in small houses, a large modern school, the Sivuqaq Inn where we stayed (a double-wing barracks of sorts with a central kitchen and small deli), and facilities for power generation and the airstrip. The natives live partly by subsistence fishing and whaling (two White Wagtails had taken up residence inside the mostly decomposed head of a whale near the boat racks) and also produce excellent ivory carvings, some of which were on display in the Anchorage airport when we flew home.

Gambell is also a true trans-Beringian community. On clear days we could easily see the mountain peaks of the Chukchi Peninsula in Russia less than forty miles to the northwest. The Siberian community of Providuniya lies in a fjord on that peninsula, where its air service is provided in part by Bering Air out of Nome, which suddenly did not seem so incongruous as we watched a couple of Common Ravens head out over the ocean, as if to those mountains, then think better of the idea and return. The host at Sivuqaq Inn, who uses the name Hansen in dealings with *turistas*, is married to a woman from Providuniya, and it was not a complete surprise to discover that Yupiks from both Russia and the United States are allowed to travel back and forth without visas. Such are the practicalities of life at the north end of civilization.

Finally, Gambell is a birding haven without compare. Because the northern point of St. Lawrence Island lies on the cross-water route for migrants moving east or west across the Bering Strait just to the north, it is a place of rest and refuge, especially during bad weather. The "boneyards" offer some low sheltering vegetation owing to the richness of the soil where thousands of years of discarded bones lie. Also, the island is a natural wall for migrant seabirds, which pass down both sides of the point. Common and Thick-billed Murres,

Tufted and Horned Puffins, and Crested, Parakeet, and Least Auklets all breed on the cliff near the village.

Birding at Gambell can be as relaxed or as intense as you want it to be. My own intensity level varied mainly because of the weather. In our five days there, I generally stayed in when it was very windy and rainy (mostly one day) but otherwise staggered about trying to see what could be found. Our group birded together part of the time but often scattered in different directions, trying to pry Bluethroats or Arctic Warblers out of the boneyards, chase Gray-tailed Tattlers along the lakeshore, or watch seabirds barreling by the point.

For me, the Bluethroats were the most frustrating bird at Gambell. I had no trouble seeing Arctic Warblers. Red-throated Pipits dropped from the sky all around me. Even Eastern Yellow Wagtails (eventually) came my way in varied plumages. Gray-tailed Tattlers walked purposefully through my scope field. But I eventually started calling the Bluethroats "Blurthroats" because they always flushed somewhere else and flew past me at some distance, offering superb views of the rufous color at the base of their tails and not much else. And why did they always land in the open next to Noah? I think he saw twice as many on the ground as anyone else in our group or the other tours at Gambell that week. There is no justice.

Our first day there offered the following message from Paul Lehman, the other WINGS guide present, over the radio in the afternoon: "OK, everyone, get over to the taxiway, there's a Little Bunting in the boneyard."

That is the kind of thing we were all wanting to hear, for there were fewer than twenty North American records of Little Bunting. Birders gathered from all over the village, some walking, some riding the backs of ATVs driven with gusto by the residents (the standard five dollar "taxi charge" seemed more and more reasonable as we wearied of constant walking through deep loose gravel).

And one came running. For once Noah was out of position, having gone back to the inn to change clothes. As I looked over my shoulder it was obvious that he had been caught in the middle of the process, for here he came, running flat out across the treacherous gravel for close on a quarter of a mile, in *jeans and a t-shirt*. Perhaps I failed to mention that the temperature was about forty-eight and there was a light mist, with winds at fifteen to twenty from the north? As he joined us in a spray of gravel, I was reminded of Lord Nelson, who was quoted as saying that he required no overcoat while walking the deck of his flagship in the Bay of Biscay in winter, because he was warmed by zeal for his country. After a little while Noah accepted the loan of some gloves and then a coat, but zeal for the bunting warmed him for quite some time. Oh, for the metabolism of a seventeen-year-old tennis champion.

The next day an even rarer vagrant, a probable Reed Bunting, appeared in the grasses on the west side of the village and was eventually seen by most who sought it, including some of the parlor-trolls who generally remained in the reading room at the inn except when good rarities appeared. These were mainly old Gambell hands who had been there several times, slowly padding their lists and waistlines while glancing surreptitiously at each other's optics.

Rich was our designated cook as well as hired leader, and on the first day he was embarrassed in the culinary role because most of our food had been put on the second plane for Gambell that day in order to get all nine of us onto the first plane. Unfortunately, Jackie's flight was the only plane that made it to Gambell that day before the weather closed down again. Thus there was very little for him to cook.

To make matters worse, the food that had been shipped from Arizona earlier had been badly damaged in transit, and since Rich makes a lot from scratch, that meant that we had a couple of boxes full of what would pass as seabird chum, for they had all sorts of ingredients mixed together in an unwholesome *goulash postale*. That evening the other WINGS tour helped feed us, with a few delicate murmurs of disapprobation.

The next day our major food shipment arrived as a string of planes came through. That night began a series of culinary triumphs that left the other tour groups (there were in effect four different parties at Gambell) sniffing and drooling in envy. We had the smug pleasure of offering some leftovers to other birders and visitors as the week went along. Somehow Rich's baked pork chops with herbs and apple slices were a bit more appetizing than the rice with mystery objects that they had brought.

The most abject of the other guests were two State of Alaska counselors making a regular visit to Gambell, which has a high suicide rate. Somehow owing to poor planning their own dinner consisted of nothing but platefuls of peas, a sight so esthetically troubling that I was prompted to check our supplies and offer them something from *chez Rich*. They moved with incredible speed to our sidebar.

The extraordinary dependence of Alaska on aviation was constantly apparent during our trip. For example, Nome, with a population of less than four thousand, has three jet flights a day to Anchorage and two to Kotzebue, which is about the same size as Nome. And that is just the jet service. Three regional carriers using small propeller-driven aircraft also fly between the villages in northwestern Alaska. As previously mentioned, Bering Air also flies as far as Provideniya, Russia.

Late in our stay at Gambell I was thinking about this replacement of almost all other forms of transportation with airplanes. That day had seen a steady stream of small, tough-looking planes come and go from the island, but now I was hearing something different, a sort of low purring that grew slowly louder. It was not the uncompromising growl of the B-17 I'd seen in Michigan, but something slightly more civilized. Out of the high overcast suddenly slid a medium-sized propeller-driven aircraft sporting four engines. A DC-6, a species of airplane that I did not realize was still flying. This one looked to be in fine shape and it flew very well indeed. It banked elegantly over the short chop of the Bering Sea, Siberia in the background, and landed with what turned out to be a shipment for the village store.

We said good-bye to Gambell the next day. It felt a little strange to be lining up by an empty runway, since we had really just arrived. We birded till the last minute, since the runway is right by the prolific area called the "Near Boneyard." An hour later we were back in Nome. The following day, after a couple of short, unsuccessful ptarmigan hunts, Noah, Tom, and I got to the airport (the others were not leaving until later). The 737 taxied up to the terminal and in a moment she will no doubt never forget, the flight attendant forgot to disarm the emergency chute, which deployed magnificently.

Unfortunately the facilities at Nome cannot repack such a chute, so that plane had to return to Anchorage deadhead and we had to wait for the 12:30 flight. We were able to make later connections all the way through, and finally reached Eugene near midnight, where Noah's father Bob Keefer met us in his matter-of-fact way:

"Did you have a good trip?"

The Next Bird

February 2004

The Falcated Duck has been in the pond for four days. I was up on top of Fern Ridge dam for three hours the day before. People are pouring in from all over the West. The duck had appeared a few weeks earlier for a couple of hours, then disappeared, earning it the local name "Falsehearted Duck" from grumblers who had missed the narrow window of opportunity.

The top of the dam is perhaps a quarter-mile long, with parking at both ends. The birders cluster loosely in the middle, gazing down into the pond upon which the UltraQuacker swims back and forth with a few hundred wigeon (the unexpected presence of a dozen Eurasian Wigeon hints at a wild origin for the Falcated Duck) and a scattering of Gadwall, coots, and Greater Scaup.

There is a curious antlike look to the scene. All morning a loose stream of dark dots appears at each end of the dam, slowly moving toward the center cluster. Each dot resolves upon close approach into a birder with that firm-lipped, slightly glassy-eyed Is-It-Still-There look. Every now and then some dogwalkers go by and wonder what is up, though media coverage has alerted many: almost a full page in the paper's outdoor section and at least one TV crew.

Spring will send all the ducks away—Tree Swallows are already here in numbers, with a few Violet-greens, Barns, and the usual early Rufous hummers and Turkey Vultures. But what will come next?

Early in this book I left a hypothetical teenager gazing on the murre colony at Heceta Head and the puffins of Cannon Beach. Few teenagers are so chosen, of course. The mechanisms through which a few from each year's crop of middle school students are infected with the call of the natural world are unknown. In the same school, the same class, the same family, only a few are selected by She Who Casts the Great Net. Even we who eagerly accepted the immanent strands of the silver net as it passed through us in our teens do not understand what happened, but we are glad for a lifetime.

Loye Miller referred to his career as a field researcher (primarily seeking bird fossils) as his "lifelong boyhood," and his memoir bears that title. The title remains apt today, both in the sense of adventure always available on a moment's notice, and in the fact that over 90 percent of young birders are boys. In fact, 90 percent is my own arbitrary figure for proportions that are probably even higher.

Yes, there are girls who gaze today on the great seabird colonies, the cranes of Malheur, the shorebirds of Bandon Marsh, the raptors of Wallowa County, but they are so very few. I do not think we can change this. Even recognizing the close biological relationship between teenagers and people, we must accept that there are differences in the way teenage boys and girls think, behave, and perceive the world they are in. Women are more substantially represented in the fields of professional biology and ornithology, which suggests that there are means of natural selection at work that do not unduly impede those with a serious interest in professional ornithology—women appear to make these choices a few years later in life.

Flashback: it is April 1969, and a rather geeky thirteen-year-old is watching his first Marsh Wren, a fascinating, exotic, varicolored sprite making its home in the reedy slough behind Roosevelt Junior High School. It darts between the cattails underneath the one local pair of Red-winged Blackbirds, showing just enough of itself from time to time to allow a careful user of Peterson's guide to ascertain its identity.

But it is time for school to start: the boredom, the occasional flashes of interest, the peculiar off-and-on snap of hormones adding sudden color to a tedious scene, the horror of PE class not quite imminent but waiting, waiting, waiting out there like a Red-tailed Hawk knowing the mouse has only one possible way to get from one patch of grass to the next.

2006

Where am I? What am I thinking? The slough vanishes in the green of soccer fields, the other thirteen-year-olds are all over the world now, and perhaps the ghost of PE class past was finally nailed into its crypt when I, forty pounds ago, improbably became one-half of the intramural mixed-doubles badminton champion team at the University of Oregon around 1977. And where are you, Laurel Stocker, partner in that unlikely victory?

Yet a walk across that field in 2006 leads where it did in 1969: the twelve-acre ash stand of Amazon Park, bordering Amazon Creek, a deep-sunk drainage ditch that has developed a lot of character in the intervening thirty-six years. It has grown a solid crop of willows that in 2004 for the first time in memory hosted a breeding pair of Common Yellowthroats. Two summers ago there were two Willow Flycatchers prospecting here—in the middle of residential Eugene. They did not stay, but next year they might.

At least six pairs of Song Sparrows nested along the creek last year, greeting joggers, cyclists, and birders alike with their clear trills and buzzy intermezzos. In most years there are two pairs of Bewick's Wrens, at least a couple of pairs of Black-capped Chickadees, and several robins nesting in the woods. I have suspected Spotted Towhee of breeding but they can get secretive in summer and I have not seen young. Downy Woodpecker is a possible breeder as well. Best of all, in many years a pair of Green Herons nests here.

I first found young Green Herons clustered in the center of the ash stand, all staring at me with mixed revulsion and uncertainty, in 1973. A young Green Heron, one of the gawkiest, most ill-constructed, down-sprouting monstrosities in Class Aves, has little excuse to be revolted by another creature, even a teenager.

I was a student at South Eugene High School then, having migrated rapidly to and from Nyssa and Cottage Grove and ended up right back where I had come from in Eugene. A very tolerant science teacher, Jack O'Donnell, realized that I would get far more out of birds than out of certain technical requirements of the high school curriculum, and allowed me to earn some credit by studying the birds of Amazon Park.

And what birds they were. This little creek and its adjacent ash monoculture hosted such gems as Cinnamon Teal and Wrentit, migrant warblers and vireos, and the exotic Green Herons. Green Heron was a less-widespread bird in the early 1970s than it is today in western Oregon—in 1940, Gabrielson and Jewett's *Birds of Oregon* called it "a decided rarity."

The nearby open parts of the park—grassy areas with a few trees— hosted a Northern Shrike one winter, perhaps the only one inside the city limits, though one winter I found one chasing House Sparrows around a residential neighborhood in northwest Eugene. Sayre once found a small flock of Least Sandpipers running about on the freshly watered baseball diamond, and on one memorable day found a singing Sage Sparrow—very rare in western Oregon—buzzing away from the same field's wire-mesh backstop.

Thirty years after I first found those young Green Herons, I still see them fly by on occasion, and sometimes hear their raucous "skrowk!," because today my home lies only one block from the park. I live about five blocks from where that thirteen-year-old—what has become of him?—watched with fascination the antics of his first Marsh Wren.

Home birds

It is a quiet day in early winter. Yesterday I covered the metal pole holding up one of my feeders with heavy bacon grease, a side benefit for my feeder birds of my Atkins-like diet. As I watch, the squirrel whose depredations I had greased against got halfway up the pole before its weight and warmth did the trick. One of the more ludicrous sights I have ever had at my feeder, the squirrel slid very slowly downward while simultaneously licking and nibbling at the larger chunks of grease. So eventually it will eat its way to the top, I sighed. Perhaps I'd better go back to using Preparation H on the pole.

From my window I can see the cluster of feeders, where goldfinches of two kinds, House Finches, and Black-capped Chickadees argue over visiting rights to the seed feeders. A Downy Woodpecker checks the suet feeder. A Western Scrub-Jay comes in for a quick seed raid. A flicker lands on the edge of the bird bath, stares into it with uncertainty, and opts out, pitching across the street to a birch tree.

These are common birds, simple birds, if you will, of which I have seen thousands. They pose no special problems in identification, they hold no exalted place on a list. They are, at this season, all rather plain-looking and they are not making any exotic sounds.

So why am I watching them? Because birding, ultimately, is not really about keeping lists—"bird golf"—but rather about awareness. I am an avid list-keeper and always have been, occasionally chasing a rarity clear across the state. Yet today I am content to watch the goldfinches squabble over who gets what seeds, even though I could be at Fern Ridge in half an hour, hoping for something more interesting.

More interesting. What does that really mean? Sure, I'd love to have a Kentucky Warbler grace my yard list, but would it be more interesting in some absolute sense? I think not. Loren Eiseley wrote of the landscape of singing sparrows and fiddling crickets as having such extraordinary depth that humanity cannot really understand it fully no matter how many layers of complexity we peel back.

A friend of mine is a professional remover of layers. Heidi Schellman, once my youthful birding partner around Eugene and in eastern Oregon, is now a physics professor and dean at Northwestern University and a quark jockey at Fermilab, riding herd on a swarm of leptons, gluons, and miscellaneous Forces in her day job while maintaining the Fermilab bird list on the side. My visiting goldfinches are composed of these same particles, all of which race about in a complex pattern that eventually builds a construct that means "goldfinch" to my eye (and apparently Edible, Peel Before Eating, to the eyes of my neighbor's cats).

There are many kinds of knowledge and many levels of awareness. In my life I am fortunate that at a young age I was introduced to the atomic swirls called birds, which have given me so much pleasure over the years, and which have added a layer of awareness to my daily life that would not have been there otherwise.

I am always looking for the next bird, not necessarily the rarest or most colorful, just the next one, as a confirmation of the inexplicable glory of life. I cannot see the molecules, atoms, and particles that make up these glorious creatures, but because of birds I can see into another dimension. I cannot ask more.

Epilogue: Germany 1944/Oregon 2002

Tod und Verklärung

Dave Marshall met Hendrik Herlyn during the *Birds of Oregon* book project of 1998-2003. Hendrik wrote the White-crowned Sparrow account. Dave was the senior editor.

At one point, Dave's background as a nineteen-year-old ball-turret gunner in B-17s over Germany during the closing years of World War Two was mentioned. Hendrik, with a twinkle in his eye as is often the case, said that his father had been among the teenage conscripts brought in late in the war to operate antiaircraft batteries for the Wehrmacht.

It is entirely possible that Dave Marshall's B-17 and Habbo Herlyn's battery exchanged ordnance, just as Richard Hugo's bomber rained bombs on the five-year-old Charles Simic as he dashed through the streets of Belgrade, a happening which they later discussed over a San Francisco lunch in 1972 as two of America's most respected poets.

In September 2002, Habbo and Elisabeth Herlyn made their second visit to Malheur National Wildlife Refuge, all the way from Germany, guided by their son.

Acknowledgements

Thanks

Most of all I must acknowledge the inspiration of my birding friends. Some of them have been friends for decades and always will be. Some are no longer living. Some have, in the natural course of living their own lives, moved out of mine, or I out of theirs. To a couple I owe apologies of one kind or another that have not been made—*yet*—to my sorrow. To all of them, I say thank you.

To my late mother, Lona Barker Contreras, I owe my life and much of what has been good in it, including the ability to go birding in my childhood, which she supported through many sacrifices. Many young birders of the 1970s remember those Malheur trips with "Wol" in our station wagon that she once drove from Cottage Grove to Eugene at ninety mph just to see what it felt like. We made pretty good time to Malheur, too.

To my late father, Albert Stephen Contreras, I owe my life and thanks for many special trips of my youth, including my first trip to Crater Lake, our walk on the deck of the *U.S.S. Missouri* at Bremerton, Washington, and our ride on the last run of the Astoria-Megler ferry when the Columbia River bridge opened.

To my brother John, who had to put up with the imperfections of my youth (and still puts up with the many that have carried over into middle age), I offer thanks for the incomparable friendship he has offered me for many years.

Some details of the 1976 Big Day were provided by Sayre Greenfield, who has always kept better notes that I do.

Daniel Farrar assisted in preparing the material from my atlasing journals and other portions of the book. Hendrik Herlyn, Donna Lusthoff, Mike Patterson, and Owen Schmidt assisted with providing facts I had managed to mislay. Thanks to Owen for providing historic material from *Oregon Birds*, which he ably edited for many years.

Thanks to Eric Horvath for permission to use his photograph of the Eurasian Dotterel.

Thanks to Hendrik Herlyn for preparing the indexed list of visited sites and Web-based information, and for updating the bird names included in the original to reflect taxonomic standards as of summer 2008. One consequence of writing fourteen drafts of a book over a four-year period is that the story can be outpaced by time.

Thanks to the staff of OSU Press, in particular Mary Braun, Jo Alexander, and Tom Booth, for their willingness to put up with this project, their willingness to tell me what was wrong with earlier drafts (there was plenty), and, ultimately their support of its publication. Several anonymous reviewers provided feedback on two drafts of the book. A number of changes, which I trust will be considered improvements, resulted from their comments.

Derivations

The quotation from David Hedges' "Steens Mountain Sunrise," is from the poem and chapbook by the same title, issued by Sweetbriar, 2003. Used by permission of the poet.

The Lane County Big Day story appeared in a slightly different form in *Oregon Birds* 26:132-35, 2000.

The Grimaldo family story "From the other side of time" appeared in a different form in *Pacesetter*, the newsletter of the Oregon Community College Association, in August 1993.

My poems "Malheur at Fourteen," "Kiger Gorge," and "Steens Mountain" appeared in the poetry chapbook *Fieldwork*, issued as a benefit for the Malheur Field Station. "Fieldwork," from which the summer weed-hoeing quotation is taken, appeared there in a different form. The quotation regarding Madonna's castle is from my poem "Revelation." All of these poems appeared in final form in my collection *Night Crossing* (CraneDance, 2004).

Portions of the Dotterel account first appeared in a more technical form as "First record of Eurasian Dotterel for Oregon" (with H. Herlyn, D. DeWitt, and L. Bloch) in *Oregon Birds* 27:9-11.

Portions of the Smith's Longspur segment were based on the details written by Hendrik Herlyn that appeared in *Oregon Birds* 27: 12.

"Why I'm not chummy with pelagic birds" first appeared in a slightly different form in *Oregon Birds* 14(2): 145, 1988.

"When the gales of November come early" is a quotation from *The Wreck of the Edmund Fitzgerald*, a splendid song by Gordon Lightfoot.

For a wonderful account of early birding adventure, see Dave Marshall's "At Malheur in 1939 with Stanley G. Jewett," *Oregon Birds* 19:11 (1993). Details of Dave's trip were taken from this source.

Tod und Verklärung (Death and Transfiguration) is a phrase perhaps best known from Richard Strauss's tone poem of that name. The poet who wrote a poem by the name is Alexander Ritter.

Recommended Reading

Ashworth, William. *The Wallowas: Coming of Age in the Wilderness.* 1978. Corvallis: Oregon State University Press, Northwest Reprints Series. 1998

Cotton, Sam. *Stories of Nehalem.* 1915. Out of print. M. A. Donohue, Chicago.

Douglas, William O. 1950. *Of Men and Mountains.* Harper, New York.

Eaton, Walter Prichard. *Skyline Camps.* 1922. Out of print. W. A. Wilde.

Kofalk, Harriet. *No Woman Tenderfoot: Florence Merriam Bailey, Pioneer Naturalist.* College Station: Texas A&M University Press, 1989.

Miller, Loye. *Lifelong Boyhood.* 1953. Out of print. University of California Press.

Sharp, Dallas Lore. *Where Rolls the Oregon.* 1912/1914, Houghton Mifflin. Out of print but reissued in 2001 as *Eastern Naturalist in the West* edited by Worth Mathewson, Sand Lake Press, Sheridan, Oregon.

Principal Locations Mentioned in the Text

This section is intended to assist people who may have an interest in visiting some of the areas mentioned, or in becoming involved in conservation efforts related to the sites. Sites not in Oregon are listed with the state.

Baskett Slough National Wildlife Refuge: http://www.fws.gov/willamettevalley/baskett/index.html • http://www.fws.gov/refuges/profiles/index.cfm?id=13587

Boiler Bay: http://www.oregonstateparks.org/park_213.php

Brownie Basin: http://www.fs.fed.us/r6/w-w/recreation/trails-ec/1651_1659_bowman_chimney_106.shtml

California Gulch, AZ: http://www.aztrogon.com/AZInfo/Location%20Details/SEAZ/CAgulch.htm

"Calliope Crossing": http://www.ecbcbirds.org/BirdingSites/Deschutes/tabid/89/Default.aspx (Item 8)

Chukar Park, Malheur County: http://oregon.hometownlocator.com/maps/feature-map,ftc,2,fid,1157283,n,Chukar%20Park.cfm

Cold Springs Campground: http://www.fs.fed.us/r6/centraloregon/recreation/campgrounds/coldsprings.shtml

Crater Lake: http://www.nps.gov/crla/

Fern Ridge Reservoir: http://www.dfw.state.or.us/wildlifearea/fernridge.htm

Fields Oasis: http://www.southernoregon.com/fields/index.html • Desert trails of that area www.thedeserttrail.org

Fort Rock: http://www.oregonstateparks.org/park_40.php

French Joe Canyon, AZ: http://www.azcentral.com/travel/hiking/articles/ french.html

Gambell, AK: See information for Nome birds. Also, for a list of major birding tour companies covering Alaska, see the Nome birds site.

High Island, TX: http://www.texasbirding.net/location.htm#high-island

Indian Ford Campground: http://www.fs.fed.us/r6/centraloregon/ recreation/campgrounds/indianford.shtml

Jefferson Park: http://www.fs.fed.us/r6/willamette/recreation/tripplanning/ wilderness/mtjefferson.html • http://www.fs.fed.us/r6/willamette/ recreation/tripplanning/trails/mtjeffersonpark/index.html

Little Belknap Crater, Melakwa Lake: http://www.fs.fed.us/r6/willamette/ recreation/tripplanning/wilderness/threesisters.html

Lost Maples State Park, TX: http://www.tpwd.state.tx.us/spdest/findadest/ parks/lost_maples/

Lostine Valley: http://www.fs.fed.us/r6/w-w/recreation/wilderness/ecwild. shtml

Madera Canyon, Florida Wash, AZ: http://www.fs.fed.us/r3/coronado/ forest/recreation/camping/sites/madera.shtml • http://www. birdingamerica.com/Arizona/maderacanyon.htm • http://www.sabo. org/birding/santa.htm

Malheur Field Station: http://www.malheurfieldstation.org/

Malheur National Wildlife Refuge: http://www.fws.gov/malheur/ • http:// www.fws.gov/refuges/profiles/index.cfm?id=13588

Miller Canyon, AZ: http://www.trails.com/tcatalog_trail. asp?trailid=HGS226-025

Nome, AK (Teller Road, Safety Sound): http://www.nomealaska.org • http://www.nomealaska.org/vc/roads.htm • http://www.nomealaska. org/vc/birds.htm

Rio Grande Valley, TX (Santa Ana): http://www.fws.gov/Refuges/profiles/ index.cfm?id=21551 •http://www.fws.gov/SOUTHWEST/REFUGES/ texas/santana.html

Siltcoos River trail: http://www.fs.fed.us/r6/siuslaw/recreation/ tripplanning/florcoos/trails/tsiltcoos1395.shtml

South Jetty Florence-Deflation Plain: http://www.fs.fed.us/r6/siuslaw/ recreation/tripplanning/oregondunes/

Steens Mountain: http://www.blm.gov/or/districts/burns/index. php • http://donb.furfly.net/malheur/places/steens.html • www. steensmountain.com • http://www.harneycounty.com/SteensMtn.htm (also includes information for Fish Lake, Jackman Park, Kiger Gorge

Succor Creek, Malheur County: http://www.oregonstateparks.org/park_13. php • http://www.blm.gov/or/districts/vale/index.php

Three Arch Rocks: http://www.fws.gov/oregoncoast/3archrocks/index. htm

Index

A

Alvadore (Oregon), 91
Alvord Desert, 11, 55, 58
Amazon Creek, 19, 130
Amazon Park, 130, 131
Anchorage (Alaska), 119, 128
Auklet: Cassin's, 50; Crested, 126; Least, 126; Parakeet, 126; Rhinoceros, 52, 93
Avocet, American, 31, 32

B

Baker Beach, 92
Baker City, 82
Baker County, 14, 82
Bandon (Oregon), 99
Bandon Marsh, 130
Barrow (Alaska), 122
Baskett Slough NWR, 11
Beardless-Tyrannulet, Northern, 80
Becard, Rose-throated, 80
Bend (Oregon), 35, 36, 67
Benson Boat Landing, 53
Benson Pond, 39
Bering Sea, 128; Bering Strait, 125
Beulah (Oregon), 86, 89: Beulah Reservoir, 86, 88
Big Indian Gorge, 58
Big Lake, 53
Bill Williams River Wildlife Area, 76
Bittern, American, 92
Blackbird: Red-winged, 130; Rusty, 11; Yellow-headed, 88, 93
Blitzen Valley, 54, 55
Blue Mountains, 66 69, 72, 74
Bluebird, Western, 16, 17, 95, 96
Bluethroat, 126
Bobolink, 82
Bobwhite, Northern, 14, 22, 30
Boiler Bay, 51
Bowman Creek, 71, 72
Brogan (Oregon), 84, 86, 89
Broken Top, 65
Brooks Range, 122
Brothers (Oregon), 64
Brownie Basin, 70, 71, 72
Brownsville (Texas), 103
Buchanan (Oregon), 88

Bufflehead, 92
Bullfinch, 17, 123
Bully Creek Road, 86
Bunting: Indigo, 109; Lazuli, 83, 95, 98; Little, 126; Painted, 109; Reed, 127; Snow, 73; Varied, 80, 102
Burns (Oregon), 35, 36, 86
Burnt River: Canyon, 82; Mountains, 84; Valley, 99
Bushtit, 62, 63, 64, 76, 77

C

California Gulch, 100, 101, 114
Calliope Crossing, 75
Camp Melakwa, 45
Cannon Beach, 129
Cantrell Road, 94
Canvasback, 96
Cape Blanco, 48
Cape Creek, 93
Cape Meares, 20
Caracara, Crested, 107
Cascade Range, 51, 62, 65, 66, 67, 68, 76
Catbird, Gray, 71
Catlow Valley, 84, 86
Chat, Yellow-breasted, 83, 88, 89
Chemult (Oregon), 61
Chickadee: Black-capped, 131, 132; Chestnut-backed, 47, 74, 91, 100; Mexican, 100, 114; Mountain, 47
Chiricahuas, 114
Chukar, 22, 87, 120
Chukar Park, 88
Chukchi Peninsula, 125
Coast Range, 48, 53, 91, 93, 99
Coburg (Oregon), 96
Colorado River Valley, 76
Coos Bay (Oregon), 48, 111
Cormorant, 22: Brandt's, 93
Corpus Christi (Texas), 103
Corvallis (Oregon), 52
Cottage Grove (Oregon), 32, 131
Cove (Oregon), 84
Coyote Creek, 94
Crane (Oregon), 86, 88
Crane, Sandhill, 32
Crater Lake, 59, 60, 61, 62, 135
Creston (Oregon), 86
Creswell (Oregon), 95

D
Dallas (Oregon), 14, 20
Davis Lake, 51
Deadwood (Oregon), 99
Devil's Elbow State Park, 92
Diamond Peak, 65
Dipper, American, 62, 63, 93, 98
Donner und Blitzen River, 31
Dotterel, Eurasian, 113, 135
Dove, White-winged, 76
Dowitcher, 122: Long-billed, 95, 99;
    Short-billed, 91
Drewsey (Oregon), 86
Duck: Falcated, 11, 129; Harlequin,
    121; Muscovy, 108; Ring-necked,
    88; Ruddy, 88, 95
Dunlin, 95, 99
Durbin Creek, 84
Durkee (Oregon), 82

E
Eagle: Bald, 16, 22, 73, 94; Golden,
    26, 73
Edwards Plateau, 105
Egret, Great, 88
Eider: Common, 122; King, 122
Eldorado (Oregon), 82
Eugene (Oregon), 14, 16, 18, 20, 52,
    53, 91, 94, 114, 119, 122, 128,
    131, 133

F
Falcon: Peregrine, 98; Prairie, 26
Farallon Islands, 104
Fern Ridge Dam and Reservoir, 11,
    18, 48, 49, 50, 51, 94, 96, 129, 132
Fields Oasis, 11
Finch, House,132
Fish Lake Campground, 56
Flicker: 132; Red-shafted, 16
Florence (Oregon), 52, 53, 109, 112
Florida Wash, 77, 78
Flycatcher: Brown-crested, 76;
    Cordilleran, 82, 83; Dusky, 27, 99;
    Hammond's, 82, 94, 98, 99; Olive-
    sided, 98; Pacific-slope, 94, 98;
    Scissor-tailed, 104, 106; Sulphur-
    bellied, 77; Vermilion, 75; Western,
    83, 100; Willow, 82, 100, 131
Fort Boise (Idaho), 31
Fort Klamath , 66
Fort Rock, 26, 27

French Joe Canyon, 114
Frenchglen (Oregon), 34, 39
Fulmar, Northern, 50, 51

G
Gadwall, 88, 98, 129
Gambell (Alaska), 119, 120, 123,
    125, 126, 127, 128
Gnatcatcher, Black-tailed, 102
Godwit: Bar-tailed, 48, 122;
    Hudsonian, 112
Golden-Plover: American, 112;
    Pacific, 112
Goldeneye: Barrow's, 25, 47;
    Common, 25
Goldfinch, 132, 133: American, 96;
    Lesser, 94, 96
Goose: Canada, 25, 98; White-
    fronted, 112
Goshawk, Northern, 56, 70
Grant County, 82
Grebe: Clark's, 93; Western, 88
Greenleaf (Oregon), 99
Grosbeak: Black-headed, 98, 100;
    Evening, 47, 100; Pine, 70, 71;
    Yellow, 80
Grouse: Ruffed, 70; Sage, 55, 87;
    Sharp-tailed, 14, 87; Spruce, 70,
    71, 73
Guillemot, 22: Pigeon, 93
Gull: Bonaparte's, 49; California, 111;
    Heermann's , 111; Herring, 92;
    Ring-billed, 93; Sabine's, 50, 51;
    Western, 91, 111
Gyrfalcon, 46, 73, 121

H
Harney Basin and Lake, 31, 86
Harper (Oregon), 86
Harrier, Northern, 56
Hawk: Broad-winged, 108; Cooper's,
    95; Gray, 102, 108; Red-
    shouldered, 94, 98; Red-tailed56,
    73, 88, 93, 130; Rough-legged, 56,
    73; Sharp-shinned, 93; Swainson's,
    18, 88
Hawk-Owl, Northern, 73
Haystack Reservoir, 19, 51
Haystack Rock, 22
Heceta Head, 53, 129
Hell's Canyon, 69
Hendricks Park, 16, 17

Heron: Great Blue, 17; Green, 94, 131, 132
High Island, 108, 109, 115
Hoodoo Butte, 53
Houston (Texas), 104
Hummingbird: Allen's, 74; Anna's, 19, 77, 81, 94; Black-chinned, 61; Broad-billed, 77; Broad-tailed, 57, 61; Calliope, 57, 61, 75, 94; Magnificent, 27, 77; Ruby-throated, 74; Rufous, 52, 56, 57, 61, 62, 74, 129; Violet-crowned, 80

I
Ibis: White, 100; White-faced, 53
Imnaha Valley, 71
Ironside (Oregon), 89: Ironside Mountain, 82

J
Jackman Park, 56
Jaeger: Long-tailed, 50, 51; Parasitic, 50, 51; Pomarine, 49, 50
Jay: Blue, 17; Brown, 107; Gray, 47, 60, 61, 98, 100; Green, 108; Steller's, 17, 47, 100
Jefferson County, 68
Jefferson Park, 66, 67, 68, 69, 71
John Day (Oregon), 82, 84
Jordan Valley, 29
Joseph (Oregon), 69
Junco, 68, 71, 72: Dark-eyed, 79; Yellow-eyed, 79
Juntura (Oregon), 87, 88, 89

K
Kerrville (Texas), 105
Kestrel, American, 94
Kiger Gorge, 57, 58
Killdeer, 95
Kingbird: Thick-billed, 80; Western, 87, 89, 94, 96
Kingfisher, 92, 96, 98, 110: Belted, 95, 108; Green, 106; Ringed, 108
Kinglet: Golden-crowned, 92; Ruby-crowned, 37
Kiskadee, 108
Kite: Hook-billed, 108; White-tailed, 18
Kittiwake, Black-legged, 50
Klamath Lake, Upper, 72
Kotzebue (Alaska), 119, 128

L
La Grande (Oregon), 74
Ladd Canyon, 84
Lake Creek, 99
Lake County, 26
Lake Havasu City (Arizona), 76, 77
Lane County, 44, 51, 90, 99
Lark, Horned, 30, 88
Leslie Gulch, 25, 27, 28, 87
Lick Creek Guard Station, 70
Little Belknap Crater, 44
Little Blitzen, 58
Long Tom River, 96
Longspur: Lapland, 92, 111; Smith's, 111
Lookout Mountain , 14
Loon: Common, 17; Red-throated; 92
Lost Maples State Park, 105, 106
Lostine (Oregon), 70: Lostine Canyon, 71; Lostine Valley, 69, 70

M
Madera Canyon, 77, 118
Magpie, 87: Yellow-billed, 81
Mahogany Mountain, 27
Malheur County, 29, 88
Malheur Lake, 31, 53
Malheur NWR, 29, 31, 32, 33, 34, 36, 37, 40, 42, 43, 51, 52, 53, 54, 107, 130, 134: Field Station, 42, 43, 88; Headquarters, 11, 36, 37, 43, 88 Malheur River and Valley, 84, 86, 89
Mallard, 25, 88
Manzanita (Oregon), 12, 13
Mapleton (Oregon), 92
McKenzie Pass, 44
McKenzie River, 63, 96
Meadowlark, Western, 94, 112
Medford (Oregon), 76
Melakwa Lake, 46, 47
Merganser: Common, 26, 99; Hooded, 98
Merlin, 26, 110
Miller Canyon, 114, 117, 118
Monument (Oregon), 82
Mt. Bachelor , 65
Mt. Fanny, 84
Mt. Hood, 45
Mt. Jefferson, 45, 65, 67: Wilderness, 66

Mt. Pisgah, 95
Mt. Rainier, 59
Mt. Washington, 45, 54, 65
Murre: Common, 22, 125, 129;
   Thick-billed, 125
Murrelet, Marbled, 92

N
Neahkahnie (Oregon), 12: Mountain,
   12, 13, 14
Neal's Lodge Resort, 106
Needles (California), 81
Nehalem (Oregon), 12
Nighthawk: Common, 33, 87; Lesser,
   77
Night-Heron, Black-crowned, 103
Nightjar, Buff-collared, 78
Nogales Sewage Ponds, 80
Nome (Alaska), 119, 120, 122, 123,
   125, 128: Nome River, 122
Norton Sound, 121
Nutcracker, Clark's, 44 ,60, 61
Nuthatch: Red-breasted, 94, 99;
   White-breasted,16, 17, 89
Nyssa (Oregon), 16, 22, 23, 25, 31,
   131

O
Oakridge (Oregon), 49
Oceanside (Oregon), 20
Ontario (Oregon), 23, 89
Oriole:, Audubon's, 108; Baltimore,
   39; Bullock's, 94; Streak-backed, 37
Osprey, 88, 92
Owl: Barn. 22, 37, 91, 95, 98, 99;
   Barred, 22, 37; Boreal, 66, 67,
   68, 69; Burrowing, 53; Elf, 77;
   Flammulated, 37; Great Gray, 74;
   Great Horned, 37, 38, 53, 68, 95,
   98; Northern Saw-whet, 37, 38;
   Short-eared, 53, 95; Spotted, 22
Owyhee Canyon and River, 26, 87
Owyhee Reservoir, 27: Uplands, 26
Oystercatcher, Black, 52, 53, 93

P
Page Springs Campground, 29
Parula: Northern, 39, 88; Tropical,
   108
Partridge, Gray, 22,30, 73
Patagonia Wayside, 79

Pauraque, 108
Pelican, 51
Penny River Crossing, 120, 121
Perkins Peninsula Park, 93
Pewee, Greater, 79, 117
Phainopepla, 77, 81
Phalarope: Red-necked, 99; Wilson's,
   88, 95
Pheasant, Ring-necked, 14, 22,23,
   30, 94
Phoebe, Say's, 43
Pigeon, Band-tailed, 91, 100
Pintail, Northern, 88
Pipit: American, 23, 25, 112, 122,
   123; Buff-bellied, 112; Red-
   throated, 111, 122, 123, 126
Plover: Black-bellied, 95, 113;
   Mountain, 113; Snowy, 92, 109,
   110; Wilson's, 42
Pole Creek, 86
Poorwill, Common, 19, 78, 87
Portland (Oregon), 49, 52, 75
Powder, North (Oregon), 84
Powder River Valley, 84
Prescott (Arizona), 77
Pribilofs, 119
Princeton (Oregon), 88
Puffin: Horned, 126; Tufted, 20, 53,
   92, 126, 129
Pygmy-Owl: Ferruginous, 78;
   Northern, 74, 89, 91

Q
Quail: California, 14, 96;
   Montezuma, 100, 102, 103, 114;
   Mountain, 53, 87, 91, 99; Scaled,
   100

R
Rail, Virginia, 92
Raven, Common, 125
Red River Valley, 107
Redhead, 94
Redpoll: Common, 72; Hoary, 120
Redstart: American, 71; Painted, 78,
   79, 117
Rickreall Creek, 14
Rio Grande Valley and River, 106,
   107
River Road, 98
Riverside (Oregon), 86,87

Robin, American, 38, 55, 91, 100, 131
Rogue Valley, 61
Rosy-Finch: Black, 57, 58; Gray-crowned, 73, 121
Royal Avenue, 94,95,96, 98
Ruff, 42, 110, 112

S

Sabal Palm Grove Sanctuary, 108
Safety Sound, 120, 121, 122
Salem (Oregon), 14, 66
San Diego (California), 80
San Francisco (California), 104, 134
San Ignatia (Texas), 104
Sandpiper: Buff-breasted, 48, 112, 113; Curlew, 110, 111; Least, 95, 131; Pectoral, 111, 122; Sharp-tailed, 42, 112, 122; Spotted, 91; Stilt, 110
Sand-Plover, Lesser, 113
Santa Ana (Texas), 108
Santa Rosa Ranch, 103
Sapsucker: Red-breasted, 16, 56; Red-naped, 56; Williamson's, 89
Scaup: Greater, 129; Lesser , 88
Scoter, 75; White-winged, 49
Scott Lake, 46
Screech-Owl: Western, 29, 53, 78, 87, 98; Whiskered, 77
Scrub-Jay, Western, 132
Sea Lion Caves, 52, 93
Seedeater, White-collared, 107
Shearwater: Pink-footed, 50; Short-tailed, 49, 50; Sooty, 50
Shoveler, Northern, 88, 92
Shrike, Northern, 131
Sierra Vista (Arizona), 117
Siltcoos River, 109, 110, 111
Siskin, Pine, 47
Sisters (Oregon), 75
Siuslaw River, 99: Estuary 92, 99; North Fork, 91, 92; North Jetty, 93; South Jetty, 92
Skimmer, Black, 75
Skinner's Butte, 94
Skua, South Polar, 50
Snake River (Alaska), 120
Snake River (Oregon), 23, 30, 64
Snipe, Wilson's, 88
Solitaire, Townsend's, 55

Sonoran Desert, 78
Sora, 92
Sparrow: American Tree, 25, 73; Baird's, 101; Black-throated, 55, 101; Brewer's, 27, 68; Chipping, 93; Five-striped, 100, 101; Golden-crowned, 99; House, 17, 131; LeConte's, 101; Lincoln's, 19, 99, 101; Sage, 131; Savannah, 92, 123; Song, 100, 131; Swamp, 18; "Timberline," 68; Vesper, 94; White-crowned, 70, 134
Squaw Back Road, 76
St. Lawrence Island, 123, 125
Steens Mountain, 42, 43, 54, 55, 56, 57, 59, 61
Stewart Pond, 94
Stilt, Black-necked, 31,32, 88
Stinkwater Creek, 88
Storm-Petrel: Fork-tailed, 50; Leach's, 48, 49, 50, 51
Succor Creek, 25, 26, 27
Summer Lake, 53
Surfbird, 52, 92, 99
Sutton Lake, 92
Swallow: Barn, 43, 87, 100, 129; Cliff, 43, 87; Tree, 40, 100, 129; Violet-green, 16, 18, 53, 87, 99, 129
Swan, Trumpeter, 39
Swisshome (Oregon), 100
Swift: Black, 93, 96; Chimney, 111; Vaux's, 16, 47, 82; White-throated, 26, 27, 82, 83, 87

T

Tanager: Flame-colored, 77, 117, 118; Hepatic, 77; Summer, 39; Western, 37, 38,117, 118
Tattler: Gray-tailed, 126; Wandering, 92
Teal: Blue-winged, 88; Cinnamon, 88, 131; Green-winged, 25, 88, 94, 95
Teller Road, 120
Telocaset (Oregon), 84
Tern: Arctic, 50; Black, 32, 94; Forster's, 88
Texas Hill Country, 105
Thrasher: Brown, 109; Sage, 23, 33, 43
Three Arch Rocks, 20, 22

Three Sisters, 44, 47, 64
Three-fingered Jack, 54, 65
Thrush: Gray-cheeked, 120; Hermit,
    47, 68, 70,71, 94; Swainson's,
    53,91, 98, 100
Tillamook (Oregon), 52
Tit: Blue, 17; Great, 17
Titmouse, Bridled, 78
Towhee: California, 19; Green-tailed,
    89, 90; Spotted, 89, 90, 91, 100,
    131
Trogon, 78, 79
Tucson (Arizona), 75, 101
Turkey, Wild, 96, 103
Turnstone: Black, 52, 92, 99; Ruddy,
    93

U
Union County, 73, 84
Unity (Oregon), 82, 83

V
Vale (Oregon), 86, 87
Vancouver, B.C., 17
Veery, 71
Verdin, 76, 77
Vireo: Bell's, 11; Black-capped, 106;
    Blue-headed, 118; Cassin's, 94, 98,
    118; Hutton's, 94; Plumbeous, 118;
    Red-eyed, 71; Warbling, 89, 98,
    100; Yellow-throated, 37
Vulture, Turkey, 129

W
Wagtail: Eastern Yellow, 110, 126;
    Wagtail, White, 125
Wallowa County, 69,71, 73, 74, 130
Wallowa Lake State Park, 74
Wallowa Mountains, 54, 59, 66, 69,
    70
Wallowa Valley, 69
Warbler: Arctic, 121, 126; Bay-
    breasted, 34; Black-throated Gray,
    27; Black-throated Green, 109;
    Cape May, 39; Chestnut-sided,
    34, 39; Golden-cheeked, 104, 106;
    Golden-winged, 109; Grace's, 78;
    Hermit, 98, 100; Kentucky, 132;
    MacGillivray's, 91; Mourning,
    39; Nashville, 72, 95, 98; Olive,
    100; Prairie, 39, 40; Red-faced,

78, 117; Rufous-capped, 114, 115;
    Townsend's, 71, 98, 106; Virginia's,
    77; Wilson's, 100; Worm-eating,
    11, 37; Yellow, 40; Yellow-rumped
    ("Audubon's"), 16, 122
Warm Springs Creek, 88
Warm Springs Indian Reservation, 67
Washburn Park, 16,17
Waterthrush, Northern, 120
Watson (Oregon), 87
Waxwing: Bohemian, 16, 73; Cedar,
    16, 17 96, 99, 100
Westfall (Oregon), 86
Wheatear, Northern, 120
Whimbrel, 49, 53
Whistling-Duck, Black-bellied, 80
Whitehorse Ranch , 55
Wigeon: American, 88, 94, 98, 119;
    Eurasian, 11, 129
Willamette Valley and River, 14, 30,
    32, 48, 51, 90, 96
Willet, 32
Willow Creek, 89, 90: Willow Creek
    Valley, 84, 86
Woodpecker: Acorn, 94; American
    Three-toed, 46; Arizona, 78;
    Downy, 88, 99, 100, 131, 132;
    Gila, 76; Golden-fronted, 106;
    Hairy, 46, 100; Ladder-backed, 77;
    Lewis's, 38, 82, 83; Pileated, 46, 53,
    98, 99
Wood-Pewee, Western, 89, 95
Wren: Bewick's, 16, 100, 131;
    Canyon, 26, 36, 76; House, 56, 94;
    Marsh, 19, 27, 39, 130, 131; Rock,
    26, 87; Winter, 50, 100
Wrentit, 99, 100, 110, 131

Y
Yachats (Oregon), 52, 53
Yaquina Bay, 45
Yellowlegs, 91
Yellowthroat: Common, 39, 40, 131;
    Gray-crowned, 108

Z
Zapata (Texas), 107